SHUTTING UP

SHUTTING UP

Listening to Your Employees, Leading by Example, and Maximizing Productivity

Eric Wagner

iUniverse LLC
Bloomington

SHUTTING UP
*Listening to Your Employees, Leading by Example,
and Maximizing Productivity*

Copyright © 2013 Eric Wagner.

All rights reserved. No part of this book may be used or reproduced by any means, graphic, electronic, or mechanical, including photocopying, recording, taping or by any information storage retrieval system without the written permission of the publisher except in the case of brief quotations embodied in critical articles and reviews.

iUniverse books may be ordered through booksellers or by contacting:

iUniverse
1663 Liberty Drive
Bloomington, IN 47403
www.iuniverse.com
1-800-Authors (1-800-288-4677)

Because of the dynamic nature of the Internet, any web addresses or links contained in this book may have changed since publication and may no longer be valid. The views expressed in this work are solely those of the author and do not necessarily reflect the views of the publisher, and the publisher hereby disclaims any responsibility for them.

Any people depicted in stock imagery provided by Thinkstock are models, and such images are being used for illustrative purposes only.

Certain stock imagery © Thinkstock.

ISBN: 978-1-4759-9856-6 (sc)
ISBN: 978-1-4759-9858-0 (hc)
ISBN: 978-1-4759-9857-3 (e)

Library of Congress Control Number: 2013913007

Printed in the United States of America.

iUniverse rev. date: 08/09/13

Contents

Acknowledgments ix

Introduction: The Dingus 1

Chapter 1: Knowing When to Shut Up 13
    So Shut Up Already! 14
    Broadening the Scope 16

Chapter 2: Communicating One-On-One 17
    Inviting Communication 17
    The Conversation: One Goal, Multiple Personalities 21
    Tuning Your Leadership to the Task 32
    Continual Mentoring 35
    Communicating with Peers 40
    Communicating Upward, Summing Up, and Moving On ... 41

Chapter 3: Communicating with the Group 43
    Meetings 43
    Participating as a Contributor Instead of The Boss 51
    Presenting to the Team 59
    Departmental Meetings 66
    Moving On 69

Chapter 4: Managing Performance 71
    Formal Performance Reviews 71
    Performance Managing with Fresh Eyes 78

But He's Irreplaceable!	81
Handling Meltdowns	84
Handling Errors	89
Using Performance-Improvement Planning	90

Chapter 5: Working with the Team 93
Building the Team	93
Motivation Is Critical	96
Staying on Top of Things	101
Dealing with Team Changes	107
Resolving Cross-Team Issues	112
The Team Is Your Extended Family	114
Moving On	116

Chapter 6: Making Decisions 117
Before You Decide	117
Decision Types	123

Chapter 7: Making Estimates 127
Overestimate and Overdeliver	128
Making the Estimate	128
Supporting Your Estimate: Balancing the Variables	135

Chapter 8: Maximizing Productivity 141
But What Is This "k" Thing? Productivity!	141
Increasing k, and Doing More with Less	142
Advanced k: Productivity Equals Value	145

Chapter 9: GOOOOAAAALLLL!!!! 149
Shared Commitment to the Goal	149
Writing Goals	150
Rewarding Properly	156

Chapter 10: Maintaining Perspective 161
Keeping the Small-Company Perspective	161
Keeping Problems in Proportion	164

Chapter 11: Getting Respect 167
    Let Your Team Find Solutions 167
    Take Responsibility 169
    Be Positively Predictable 171
    Follow the Rules 173
    Sucking It Up: Selling a Management Decision 175
    Assume Nothing Stays Secret 178
    Getting Respect from the Boss 184

Chapter 12: Managing the Boss 185
    Learning His Communication Style 185
    Surprise! Here's a Blindside! 187
    Making Complaints 189
    Don't Save the Punch Line 189
    Be Positive 190
    In Boss We Trust 191
    Lookin' Good 192
    Moving On 193

Chapter 13: Beyond the Team 195
    Making a Good First Impression 195
    You Know That I Know That You Know 197
    Dealing with Grenade Throwers 198
    Communicating with Customers 200
    Human Resources 206
    The Offshoring Cycle 207
    The Consultant Conundrum 212

Chapter 14: Summing It All Up 215

Acknowledgments

I would like to thank the many people who contributed to this book, most of whom will have no idea that they've done so. To all the lousy management people I've worked with, or worked for: thanks for showing me what not to do. And to those truly talented managers—and most of you do know who you are: thank you for the good example and for giving me the template upon which I could build my own personal style.

But mostly, thank you to my family and closest friends for your support, companionship, and humor—a quality I treasure most of all. To Lauren and Adam: nobody could ask for better kids. To Bob, Sheilah, and Matthew: nobody has ever had better parents or a better brother. And for Rebecca: nobody could have asked for a better editor … or wife.

Introduction: The Dingus

Everybody knows a Dingus or two. They're everywhere. Maybe you don't know them, per se (who would want to?), but you run into them all the time—stuck behind them in line at the supermarket or the bank, witnessing their antics as you drive to work, or sitting next to them on an interminable airplane ride. As much of a pain as they can be, they often provide moments of twisted entertainment as well—stories for a buddy over lunch or the family after work.

They happen. They're part of the equation of life. Fine.

Until you have to work for one.

Now, one of life's simple displeasures morphs into something else.

Maybe it's not too bad. Maybe your Dingus only makes your job a little more difficult, or he never heard the saying that "you have two ears and only one mouth for a reason." Maybe it's a little worse: he stands between you and a more satisfying career, or he casts a heavy shadow over what would otherwise be a happy day-to-day experience. Maybe you can basically deal with him, but you think he's a moron—incapable of analyzing situations, making decisions, or communicating his thoughts clearly. Maybe you simply have no respect for him whatsoever.

But maybe he awakens a frequent desire to use a ball-peen hammer to drive an ice pick through your right ear, mercifully ending the torture that is your 9-to-5 weekday experience …

Worked for one of these? So have I—more than I care to remember. But I did remember, and I accumulated my share of stories over time, mentally filing them away under "Dingus 101." As I advanced through my career, understanding how to deal with the occasional Dingus became a part of my professional playbook. Past Dingus experience made handling each new Dingus easier, and—equally importantly—helped keep me from becoming one myself.

As I said, they were just part of the equation of life. And life went on.

But then my wife began relating stories about her new boss. She had been lucky: she had a long-term position in a stable organization, and her working life had been largely Dingus-free. But then an acquisition placed her smack in the clutches of an epic Dingus. Listening to her fret about her first experience of this unique pleasure was both enlightening and frustrating … and morbidly fun, too.

For a year or so, we would have regular discussions about her Dingus. "Why does he keep speaking to us as if we've never done our jobs before?" "We had some great ideas to streamline our development process, but he won't listen to us." "Is this the right way for him to communicate about personnel issues?" "He's having a huge fight with the QA manager again. Can't they just figure it out and leave us out of it?" I would use my decades of management experience to help answer her questions, provide suggestions for ways to handle him through various situations, and commiserate over his more bizarre antics.

Then I found myself having more discussions with friends and other relatives who had Dingus bosses of their own. And I started to wonder: *How did these Dingus managers come to pass in the first place?* I mean, someone had to decide that these people were the best ones for the job in the first place, right? So if a particular boss didn't start out as a Dingus, how did he morph in such a tragic fashion?

Had he been badly managed himself, and was he using his own unfortunate experiences as a guide, mimicking the poor behaviors of a previous Dingus? Had he never had the privilege of working for someone who did it right, giving him a road map to follow on his own management journey? Maybe he did have that privilege, but he didn't recognize it—or for some reason it didn't match his expectations of how proper management should be done.

In short: didn't he realize there was a better way?

One of the great things about working for someone and experiencing his own particular style is that—whether it's good or bad, whether he manages by exception or micromanages, whether he helps you get around obstacles or routinely lobs hand grenades into your soup, whether he's a Dingus or not—you still learn something. Of course, what you learn is subject to your own personal skew, but you learn something nonetheless. With each new manager, you discover what you like and what you hate. You realize how it feels to be subject to each different management style, and you learn what motivates you personally to work harder and better.

When you're exposed to your own Dingus, and you recognize him for what he is, you pledge, *If I become a manager someday, I'll never be like that.* You're a better person for the realization. And conversely, when your manager has the right combination of techniques and the skill to manage well, you're ready to sacrifice your firstborn for him. You vow to remember how it felt, and to replicate it as closely as possible when you become a manager yourself.

That's exactly what I have done over the course of more than three decades in the working world—the vast majority as a manager myself. And, of course, managers have managers too. So as soon as I climbed onto that management ladder, I began gaining experience from both perspectives.

It was interesting to learn ways to deal with a Dingus, but I realized it made for an even more interesting task to consider how to avoid becoming one myself—and, granted, I did not always succeed, especially early on. More recently, I realized that, throughout my decades of management, I had not only tried to avoid being a Dingus, but I had also spent a large part of my time coaching the managers that were on my teams, trying to help them circumvent the Dark Side as well.

Over the years I developed a heck of a tool belt, fashioned from a combination of my own efforts to lead my teams and dozens of management and leadership courses. As I acquired more and more responsibility, including supervising lower-level managers who reported to me, I wanted my people to be able to benefit from my experience and stick a few of my tools into their own belts. After all, just as you learn from your own positive experiences as well as your own mistakes, you should learn from other people's experiences and mistakes too.

And the circle completes itself: in coming to understand how not to be a Dingus, you frequently gain further insight into how to deal with them as well.

Shutting Up

So where did that management tool belt come from? What has my career looked like? What experiences have led me to develop such a long list of tips and tricks?

More years ago than I care to count, I earned my BSE in Computer Science from Arizona State University and went to work as a frontline computer programmer for GTE Communications Systems in Phoenix, Arizona. Three years later, I was promoted to my first management position, where I led a group of about thirty other programmers. I'll admit I was a tad rough around the edges as a new manager with no formal training in that art. But I found that I truly enjoyed helping my workers improve themselves, both as individual programmers and as members of a collaborative team. It was at this time, teaching myself nearly as much as I was teaching my team, that the first of my personal management rules came into being. Soon, another promotion to QA Manager led to some additional new experiences. Many of these were in the general politics of management and working closely with other management-level people for the first time.

After completing my MS in Software Engineering from ASU, I moved to the San Francisco Bay Area to join Ithaca Software, a 3D graphics start-up that had recently relocated from upstate New York. As the Vice President of Development, I had far wider responsibilities than ever before. I learned how to truly lead an entire development organization. In addition to those duties, I interfaced with nondevelopment groups, met with customers, and gave numerous presentations, both internal and public. Most importantly, I got to work with an incredible group of people who showed me just how far the bar can be raised when everyone expects amazing results (shout-outs to Scott, Bob, Brian, Carl, Jeff, Milt, and Wiggy).

Three years later, Ithaca was acquired by Autodesk, who planned to build our HOOPS Graphics technology into AutoCAD, the world's leading CAD software. I was promoted to Vice President for AutoCAD Development to oversee the integration. Suddenly I had three hundred people on my team, which made for an enormous learning curve and provided me with a major opportunity to develop many more management tricks. My tenure at Autodesk saw the release of AutoCAD R14 and AutoCAD 2000, two consecutive successes that helped to restore AutoCAD's reputation as the gold standard of the CAD industry (more shout-outs to Ajay, Chris, Debbie, Kathy, Rose, JJ, Jeanne, Jen, and Carol).

In the late 1990s, Autodesk decided to try its luck in the new dot-com universe and spun out Buzzsaw.com. I was recruited to run the engineering group there, and we spent a couple of very intense years learning about the new world of hosted applications (another shout-out to Melissa). At Buzzsaw, I also got my first experience handling several acquisitions and partnering with Océ, a Dutch company that produced top-of-the-line plotters and other output devices. Sadly, our dot-com days turned dot-bomb, and Buzzsaw was reacquired by Autodesk. But during our time out on our own, we created a great product that's still in use today.

When Buzzsaw was reintegrated into the Autodesk family, our partner, Océ, acquired a part of Buzzsaw that resided back in Phoenix. Rather than return to Autodesk, I accepted Océ's offer to return to my old hometown to run the former Buzzsaw group and several other semi-independent companies that comprised Océ's US-based software operations. There was much fertile ground for fresh management experience there. For the first time, I was running full businesses and interacting with people from many different companies and multiple international divisions (another shout-out to Patty).

A few years later, I departed Océ to manage software development at GoDaddy.com. Yes, those guys. No, naked girls do *not* run through the hallways ... usually. GoDaddy was a young company still operating with the "garage band" mentality, and that's where I began to start genuinely mentoring other people who were coming fast up the management ladder. By then, I had enough management experience and tips up my sleeve that I was able to really work closely with new managers, helping them learn the ropes and avoid the pitfalls (more shout-outs to Brian, Dave, Mike, and Scott).

My penultimate stop was running another software-development shop as Chief Technology Officer for Pearson Digital Learning, a division of the world's leading academic and educational publisher. More than anywhere before, at Pearson I was able to use my rules and experiences to help some newer managers learn the ropes and navigate the management politics of a huge multinational corporation (yet more shout-outs to Andy, David, Greg, Jordi, Peter, Rajender, Ray, and Dragon).

Finally, in December 2012, I found myself with an opportunity I couldn't refuse. Through some previous contacts, I was offered the chance to hop back into start-up land as the President of MindNest, a technology incubator with not-so-secret plans to take over the world. I'm back to working with a ravenous bunch of ridiculously smart people, and still learning new things every day.

It was while I was working at Pearson that the idea for this book began to crystallize. In addition to my duties as CTO, I was recruited to spend a great deal of time on the road, giving keynote presentations on the future of technology at a wide variety of conferences, summits, and industry meetings. I was giving presentations several times per month, sometimes several per week. And for the first time I was reaching an audience beyond my own team and peers, even beyond my own company entirely. At nearly every conference I would chat with other presenters, many of whom had written books of their own and were appearing as professional speakers rather than as representatives of specific companies. They encouraged me to broaden the scope of my thoughts—rather than focusing on one group or vertical market (the Pearson audience was, of course, largely focused on education), how could my ideas be useful to the business community at large? When I mentioned that I'd been jotting down my management tips and tricks for years, the encouragement grew. And I realized it was time to pull it all together.

Why *had* I started writing down all those tips, right from the beginning of my career, whenever I learned one—or made one up? I'm still not really sure. I believe, at first, it was a way for me to refresh my own practice. When you find yourself in a situation that you've experienced before, and you've already developed a particular technique for handling it, the correct procedure usually pops into mind without much effort. But trying to recall a long list of techniques without immediate context can be a tad trickier. Having my notes right at hand made my periodic self-maintenance a little easier.

Maybe there was some subconscious thought about eventually recording my notes for posterity, as I am doing now. The most amazing thing is that they actually survived as long as they did. Over the years, they have endured the transition from simple Unix text files, through a plethora of different word-processing programs, back and forth through Google Docs and the Cloud, over what I would estimate to be at least fifteen different computer systems, and finally coming to rest on my current system of choice. I could have lost a lot of money betting they would get lost somewhere along the way. But they were valuable enough to me to make sure I kept track.

Shutting Up

When I made the decision to proceed with this book and began to go through all my notes, I was thinking that my primary audience would be people who were first starting their climb up the management ladder. And I expected to reach mostly those new managers who were operating in technical fields. Unlike in many other industries, tech companies do not usually hire new graduates (think MBAs) to fill leadership roles. Instead, they promote from within. They take their own people—the ones who exhibit exceptional performance in their own particular endeavors—and promote them to management.

And that can be a problem. Although these newly minted managers have intimate knowledge of the work that their new squad must do, they may have minimal to no experience in actual leadership. Some may have a fundamentally flawed view of what the management job even means. (I once asked an internal applicant why he wanted to be a manager. His response was "I want to be the one to approve the timesheets and expense reports.")

But whatever technical skills they may bring to the table, managers must consider themselves, first and foremost, *people* managers. One of the most egregious errors a manager can make is to limit his job to simply ensuring that the frontline work is being performed exactly the way he desires. Yes, product and process management are important parts of the job, but the people part must come first. Coaching, communicating, leading, and dealing with performance issues—these are critical tasks that should come before any technical issues.

Unfortunately, thanks to their minimal exposure to it, managing people is likely to be the job with which most new managers feel the least comfortable. That which we are uncomfortable doing tends not to get done. And that leaves a team in very poor condition.

For all these reasons, new technical managers seemed to be my target audience.

But it quickly occurred to me that I was unnecessarily limiting the scope of my expected audience. New managers were not the only people who could benefit from my experience. Indeed, even with nearly three decades of management experience behind me, I still manage to pick up new tips and tricks on occasion. We are never too old or too experienced to stop learning about the tools on someone else's tool belt—and learning how to take advantage of those tools ourselves.

In the same way, I soon realized that my own familiarity with technical fields was narrowing my intended focus needlessly. These tips do not need to be confined to the technical management space. I believe most leaders, in all industries, will find the majority of this information to be pertinent to them. Furthermore, much of this knowledge can easily apply to how we deal with other people throughout our everyday lives. Like management, life is all about dealing with people. Whether it is leading and coaching them, learning from them, or communicating with them as equals, we all manage our relationships with others every day of our lives.

I hope I'm not taking too much liberty when I say that most of the people who have worked with me have felt that I was a competent manager. No, we can't all be perfect, and I'll be the first to admit that I still fail to follow some of my own rules occasionally. But I would like to believe that, because I tried to adhere to this set of rules, my performance exceeded that which it would otherwise have been. I'd also like to believe that the coaching I have provided to the managers who have worked for me has helped them to become better leaders themselves. Many of them have gone on to higher-level positions in a number of companies. I hope they took some of these tools with them.

On the other hand, I do not assert that the topics I will discuss here comprise an all-inclusive summary of everything that a manager needs to know. This is not the manager's guide to the universe. But the subset here has served me well. It certainly works as a starting point, especially for those embarking on their management careers. Depending on your own level of experience, some of the points I discuss will be more obvious than others, and some may appear counterintuitive when I first present them. But my desire, even for those items that seem self-evident, is to add some of my own spin and seasoning.

In your own position, some of these concepts may work better than others. Some may be downright distasteful to you. I understand. It's my experience ... and my book. Your mileage may vary. One important thing I've learned is that you always have to tweak your game to fit the current circumstances. Because every situation is unique, use these items as a guide, not a straitjacket.

One final note before we begin. Throughout this book, I use the terms "he," "his," and "him" in a completely gender-neutral way. I understand that this is a potentially controversial decision, but it's a personal one. As a reader, I've always been distracted by writing that randomly toggles between the male and female forms without any apparent pattern. Worse is when an author constantly uses "he or she" and "him or her" language. And my wife, the technical writer, flatly forbade me to mix singular and plural terminology like "each person should monitor their goals" or "if you have a problem with a coworker, go talk to them." Please don't bash me for gender discrimination. My intent is only to keep the language simple, straightforward, and free of distraction. And the people who have worked with me will attest that no such bias exists.

Okay? Then let's get started. And the best place to begin is ...

Chapter 1:
Knowing When to Shut Up

We all know people who are so enamored with the sound of their own voices that it's impossible to get a word in edgewise. That's bad enough if you're trying to have an ordinary conversation, and it's worse if you're trying to collaborate with someone. So let's consider the single most important thing to do when you're communicating one-to-one, especially when you're communicating with subordinates at work: *shut up.*

What? You're the manager! That's true, and if you want to talk until the cows come home, no one who reports to you is likely to stop you. If you're trying to be an effective, *respected* manager, however, you must realize that what you have to say is much less valuable than anything your subordinates might have to say to you. But there's a problem:

People, by their nature, don't communicate.

Even under the best of circumstances, it can be incredibly difficult to get someone to open up and communicate freely. Many people have a natural distrust of their leadership that can only be overcome with many months, if not years, of positive contact. When your teams learn that you listen to them, you take their ideas to heart, you actively work to resolve their complaints, and you never simply lie to them outright, they will slowly come to trust your leadership. But this will never happen if you do not give them the opportunity to open their mouths in the first place.

So Shut Up Already!

Someone comes to you with a question, and you answer it. That seems simple enough, right? But the instinct to speak, to answer a question before it is completely asked—or before the real question has actually been asked at all—is as strong as the gravity emanating from a black hole. And just when we think we're being helpful, we're actually throwing away the most important potential of the conversation: useful feedback, a thoughtful idea, or helpful criticism. And we're quashing any chance we might have of eventually forming a trusted bond with that team member.

"But I let him ask the question!" you say. Did you really? Jumping in during (or immediately following) your visitor's initial monologue might make you feel like you've handled the situation well, but unless it really was an utterly simple question—"What time is that meeting again?"—your employee will leave your office feeling like the conversation was a waste of time. He didn't make the points he really wanted to make, and he didn't get to the true questions or problems that were bothering him.

And he isn't going to blame himself for that. He's going to blame you.

What you really need is the ability to hold your tongue. It is vital to let your employee speak until he has said everything he wants to say. When I'm having a discussion about anything even remotely more complicated than the time of day, I will usually do something to actively remind me to shut up—literally bite my tongue, sit on a hand, or clench my teeth together. I want my people to open up to me and give me all the ideas, comments, or criticisms that they have. And they'll never do it if I start "fixing" their problems before I find out what the problems really are.

One Mississippi, Two Mississippi ...

But shutting up isn't enough on its own. There's another critical element to listening: *waiting for more*. After your visitor has gotten through his points and he closes his mouth, delay opening your mouth even longer. You may find it hard to believe, but even at the point when you think it's your turn, chances are very good that your guest hasn't actually said everything on his mind. Whether it's an idea he thinks is a little too far out on the fringe, or a criticism that he thinks you might not want to hear, he hasn't brought it up yet.

This is when I use my rule of "Seven Mississippi." Yes: I literally start counting it out in my head. When you allow an awkward silence to fall over the discussion, your guest will start feeling like it's his obligation to get the dialogue going again. And then he'll start trying to figure out what the heck he can say next. Chances are, he will dive down into some of those as-yet-unsaid items he didn't cover initially. That's when he'll get to the sweet chewy center of what he really had to say in the first place.

I'll be the first to admit it: it can definitely feel a little funky to allow that silence to build over what seems like a seven-second eternity. But it's absolutely worth it when the other person starts talking again and you realize that now you're getting to the real meat of the matter.

Ask, Don't Tell

But sometimes "Seven Mississippi" isn't enough to get someone talking. Even though you've kept your mouth shut, even though you've waited, you may have the strong sensation that there is something left unsaid. In that case, you must nudge your guest to bring it out. So instead of jumping into your part of the discussion, ask a simple question that encourages your visitor to elaborate. Questions that begin with "Could you explain more about …" or "Why do you feel that …" will keep the focus on your guest, and with any luck he'll open the door to that fresh information.

I am rewarded nearly 100 percent of the time for this behavior. It's amazing how a simple clarifying question can lead to data that you never would have heard if you hadn't shut up and listened.

The Reward

It sometimes takes practice, and it always takes patience. But if you shut up long enough to *listen* long enough, and you use strategic questions to draw out more information, your people will eventually tell you whatever it is they need to say. And when they do, they will feel that the time with you was well spent. More importantly, they will want to repeat that experience in the future. And even more importantly than that, they will tell their coworkers about the experience, and that will make the rest of your team curious about trying it as well.

Broadening the Scope

Inasmuch as we are discussing shutting up with respect to dealing with our employees, we don't have to stop there. Shutting up works just as well with peers, bosses, other departments, and customers. When you use this approach on a grander scale, you will develop a reputation as someone who really listens. Others will initiate discussions with you more frequently. You'll hear more and better ideas, and you'll gather criticisms and counter-ideas that are critical for performing your duties to the best of your ability.

Active, intentional listening becomes the key foundation for many other management skills, especially …

Chapter 2: Communicating One-On-One

In this chapter, we will target some of the many different types of dialogues that happen between two people, and we'll expose how to maximize the effectiveness of each. Every situation is different, and getting the most out of each conversation requires us to pay attention and tune our actions and responses to the needs of the discussion.

Inviting Communication

Let's begin our quest for excellent one-on-one communication with a look at whether your working setup is encouraging such conversations to occur. Whether you're based in a real, private office or some sort of cube or open-office structure, you can set things up to encourage folks to communicate with you on a frequent basis. Or you can send an unintentional but clear signal that you'd really rather not be bothered.

Your Office: Location, Location, Location ...

First off, consider the actual physical placement of your office or cube. Unfortunately, this may not always be totally in your control. Sometimes, upper management likes to have all the managers sit together—maybe close to the big boss. Sure, this makes it easy for him to find you when a choking is necessary. But think about it: Are the majority of your daily communications really with your boss and peers? I would take a hard look at myself if I spent more time each day with my boss and fellow managers than I did working with my own team.

If you do have the choice, sit as close to your team as you can. The opportunities for solid, ongoing communication with your team will be vastly improved. Sitting with my team makes it easier for them to see me as *part* of the team. And when I sit with my workers, instead of my fellow managers, it sends a message to my team that they are my priority, and not the higher-ups.

Plus, it makes it much easier for my folks to quickly stop by when they need to—or even for nothing more than a friendly hello. It can be a daunting task for an employee to walk over to "management row" for a conversation. If you move yourself out of convenient reach, that distance can easily turn into a good excuse for someone to talk himself out of trying to communicate with you. And never reside on a different floor than your team. Requiring someone to walk a bit is one thing, but stairs and elevators are like barbed-wire fences.

If you happen to be high enough in the food chain to have managers reporting to you, the same rule applies. Sit them close to their people. Remember that they should be working for their own teams just as much as they work for you, and resist the temptation to suck them into your own tight orbit.

... and Layout, Layout, Layout

Beyond the location of your office, consider its arrangement as well. Way back in the 1980s, I took a tip from a character on the television show *Hill Street Blues*. Captain Frank Furillo never let his desk stand between himself and his visitors. When someone came to see him, he would stand up and walk around his desk to have the discussion face-to-face. As a brand-new manager myself, I loved that approach and took serious note of it.

Thanks to today's prefabricated office furniture and its required layouts, you may not be able to position things exactly to your liking. But if you have some flexibility, try to set yourself up so that your desk isn't positioned as a barrier to everyone who walks in. If you have room for a separate table and chairs, where you can sit down together, you're good to go. But if you have no other seating available, and you can't avoid the desk-in-the-middle setup, do your best to remove its barrier potential. When you have visitors, slide your chair over to the end of the desk, so you're talking more around the desk than over it. Folks who visit with you will feel an increased connection with you.

Distractions

There's another benefit to positioning yourself away from your desk when you're meeting with someone: you probably won't end up anywhere near your computer. Nothing says, "I'm a Dingus, and everything else I have to do is more important than anything you've got to tell me," like continuing to work or checking your email while you pretend to entertain your visitor. Even a quick glance over to your computer screen is enough to send a clear message—you'd rather watch those stock quotes stream by than focus on the conversation. Reduce the temptation to cheat by hitting the screen lock or screen-saver key when you're about to start. Then scoot away from the computer screen. Now you're telling your guest that you're really working with him right now.

And don't even think about fiddling with your cell phone!

Your Cube: Finding Privacy

If you're in a cubicle, you're located reasonably close to your workers, and you've set up the best layout you can, there's not much more you can do physically to show your team that you want to hear from them whenever they have the need. But what happens when one of your people wants to discuss a sensitive issue? It's pretty tough to have that conversation in the open-ish cube environment.

So how do you handle it? You can't require folks to schedule a formal meeting with you every time they need to handle a quick issue. As soon as you do that, you've pretty much lost the game. Instead, have a private area close by where you can retreat whenever a discussion starts turning sensitive. Fortunately, in cube-heavy office designs, there are usually a number of small conference rooms scattered around. The trick is to make sure that at least some of those rooms are *not* bookable with your company's meeting-management or calendar system. Instead, leave them perpetually free for quick, impromptu conversations, and let your people know why they're there. If your workers know that you'll be able to head to a private room when the conversation turns sensitive, they won't have any excuse not to initiate the dialogue.

Your Office: The Open Door

If you have a true office, that solves the privacy problem—you can close the door anytime. But the enhanced privacy may create other issues. Like that door itself.

Look at your office door. Is its normal position open or closed? When you enter your office, do you automatically close the door behind you? Not good! It doesn't matter if you put a sign on the door that says, "I'm always available! Enter!" It doesn't matter if your entire office is windowed and everyone can see what you're doing. That closed office door is a high-decibel announcement to your troops that will kill your communication, regardless of your intentions. If stairs and elevators between you and your team are like barbed wire, a closed door is the Berlin Wall.

Instead, leave that door open virtually all the time. Yes: even when you're working on a task that requires concentration, and you'd rather not be disturbed. It is more valuable to be disturbed by someone who has decided he wants to communicate with you. If you need privacy and concentration to finish some big project, then come in early, stay late, or lock yourself in your study at home. Your office is a place for interaction with your team, not privacy.

Of course, you can close the door when circumstances require it. If you're holding a meeting and need the privacy, or if the meeting is making too much noise and might distract the rest of your team, then by all means close it up. In general, however, remember that a closed door is a barrier to success. Keep that barrier removed whenever possible.

The Conversation: One Goal, Multiple Personalities

Working with your team, you're going to come across numerous different personalities and situations. Treating every person and conversation the same way—even two different conversations with the same person—is a recipe for disaster.

So when someone sits down in your office and the conversation starts, shut up and listen. And while you're shutting up, identify the type of situation you're in and prepare to respond accordingly.

In this section, we'll talk about a few possibilities.

The Nervous Wreck

Most of your team will become accustomed to meeting with you in your office or in some other one-on-one situation. Your boss, your peers, and your direct reports will expect to meet with you privately as a matter of course. However, if you have managers reporting to you, you will most likely have occasions when you'd like to speak privately with one of their reports.

For some of these frontline workers, going to your office for a meeting—or knowing that they'll be meeting privately with you, at your request—can be an unnerving experience. Yes, they'll get used to you eventually, but the first few times you schedule a private talk with them they're going to be really worried about what they did wrong. Depending on the circumstances, even members of your own direct team may sometimes have the jitters.

When you have a potential Nervous Wreck on your hands, you need to go out of your way to get the person comfortable—even before the meeting starts. First, when you send the meeting invitation, be clear about the purpose. Never schedule a one-on-one talk without providing an agenda. Better yet, stop by the person's cube and chat for a minute before you even send the invitation. Then let him know that you'd like to schedule an official meeting to continue the discussion.

Despite your best efforts, you won't always be able to convince people of the innocent nature of an impending meeting. Even if you're clear about the topic, people might still believe that you're diverting attention from the real reason that you want to talk— maybe it's a reprimand, or even termination! If you believe that your guest may still have some major concern, get to the subject right away. "Thanks for coming. This XYZ project really needs our attention."

The same technique is doubly important when you have to call someone in for a discussion without having a chance to set him up for it. If you call and ask him to come to your office right away, he'll be plenty sweaty when he arrives. Set him at ease as quickly as you can. "Hey! Come on in. Nothing bad is going on here. We just need to talk about the XYZ project." You will notice an immediate change in demeanor.

The Venter

It's guaranteed that your employees will get upset from time to time. Someone will show up at your door, you'll see him walking in the halls with that look on his face, or another team member will alert you that he seems to be distressed about something. Eventually, that someone will arrive in your office for a chat. The next few minutes will determine whether he gets past the problem and back to work, or he stews on it—and maybe even gets others incited and diverted from their own work.

Sometimes the item of displeasure is something that you can fully control. Sometimes it isn't. Even if you don't have the power to handle the real issue, the way in which you handle the *conversation* can go a long way toward returning the employee to a more positive state of mind.

First off, it is crucial to allow the Venter to vent without interruption. And remember that the first salvo might only scratch the surface of the deeper issue. Follow the Seven Mississippi rule—you might stretch it to Ten or Twelve Mississippi to ensure that he's gotten everything possible off his chest. Wait for it. It will come. If you try to calm someone down before he's adequately vented all his frustrations, he won't hear you at all. And he won't be ready to proceed with a productive discussion.

Remember: if you solve something that wasn't the real problem to begin with, you've wasted everyone's time.

When the venting is over, reassess. Many times, the mere act of venting itself will be cleansing, and your disgruntled employee will feel gruntled again. Great! Thank him and get back to work. But sometimes the situation will require a response from you. Once you are confident that all the issues are on the table, you can begin having a productive discussion about the situation. And because you allowed the employee to speak freely and fully at the beginning, chances are good that he'll be willing to hear what you have to say now. Still, stay alert to the possibility that there is yet more information buried even deeper, and that you may not have uncovered everything. File that knowledge away in your memory, and use it to adapt your style in future interactions with this person.

Finally, if some sort of legitimate problem emerges, determine whether there's an actionable item for you to take on. If so: by all means, do it! Seize the opportunity to turn a venting session into a positive outcome. Something will improve in the workplace, and your employee will be pleased with you. He'll also be likely to pass on his observations to his fellow workers, further gaining you trust and respect.

The Messenger

Everyone has heard the warning "Don't shoot the messenger." But when the rubber hits the road, few of us tend to actually remember it. When someone comes to you to discuss a problem—whether he is alerting you to a bad situation, or simply all-out venting about something that may or may not be under your control—never make him feel personally responsible for the mess.

This can be harder when the problem has developed because of a decision that you made or a policy that you implemented. When that happens, it can be easy to unload on the messenger in self-defense. But the minute you jump down someone's throat about a problem that isn't his personal doing, you can be sure he won't be coming back to you with similar alerts in the future.

Instead, take a breath and savor the fact that someone actually trusts and respects you enough to come talk to you about it. Remember that we, as managers, are not always right. It's a *good* thing to have your folks out there acting as real-time barometers, and even better that they're willing to speak openly with you. So instead of attacking, praise him for his act:

> "Hey, thanks for coming to me with this. I know it wasn't something you did. In fact, we both know that if anyone's at fault for this, it's me. I don't know if it was hard for you to come point this out to me, but I appreciate it. If we're going to succeed, we have to quickly adjust anything that's not working, even if that thing was created by me. Then we all look better in the end."

Now that worker won't hesitate to come to you again when he needs to.

Finally, when you announce a change you're making as the result of this kind of information, give credit where it's due. "Jeff pointed out that my decision to eliminate that extra review wasn't working so well. So now we're going to …" Acknowledging the messenger instead of shooting him will help get the word around that you appreciate that kind of feedback.

The Nibbler

Another interesting type of interaction can begin when an employee starts asking questions about company policies, procedures, and perks in a seemingly generic way. "How long does it take for someone to get promoted?" "What are the company's policies regarding merit increases and bonuses?" "How are reserved parking spaces assigned?" As the Encyclopedia Manageria that you are, you may be tempted to respond with a recitation of company policy. "Look what I know!"

But inasmuch as you think you've successfully administered the treatment, you might have completely misdiagnosed the disease. Sure, sometimes these questions really can be taken at face value, and the questioner will leave satisfied. But in many cases, the direct question itself is actually just "nibbling" around the edges of the issue. The question may be phrased as a generic query, but underneath it all, the questioner is asking something very specific about his own situation.

In the above examples, the employee might really be asking, "When will I be eligible for a promotion?" "Will I be getting a raise or bonus this year?" "Why don't I have a reserved parking spot?" He might be asking because of how someone else was treated, trying to deduce if a similar perk could be coming his way too. Or in the case of an explicit question like "How do project bonuses work?" the implicit query might really be "Why did Jack get a project bonus and I didn't?"

We have already discussed the importance of shutting up, listening carefully, and making sure that the employee has communicated everything he has to say before you start talking. But when you have a Nibbler on your hands, you must realize that the question he asked might not really be what's on his mind at all. To decipher his real concern, try to relate the explicit question to current circumstances and recent events. Take into account your previous experiences and interactions with this particular person, and then begin the discussion. Your employee will be amazed that you were able to get to the real source of his concern, and he'll be pleased to get his real questions answered. Plus, he'll come away from the discussion feeling like you really care about him personally.

By the way, don't assume that Nibbler behavior like this will happen only with younger or newer employees. I have seen this behavior from a wide range of people, including very senior and experienced workers.

Greener Pastures

Occasionally, one of your people will arrive with some chilling news: he is considering leaving the company for another position. If he has already made the decision and accepted an offer from somewhere else, all you can really do is negotiate a friendly exit. But if your employee hasn't actually accepted a new job yet, there's a good chance that he's coming to you now because he really wants your advice. This situation is uncommon, but it does happen.

Before you panic or come to any conclusions, shut up! Use the techniques we've already discussed to draw him out and figure out some possible reasons why he's considering a change. Remember that psychology can work against you. The harder you push your employee to be happy and stay, without providing any reasons to back it up, the more he will feel the need to depart. Instead, listen carefully and figure out what's going on behind the scenes.

A worker's decision to leave may not mean he has a real problem with his current job; actually, the fact that he's coming to you at all means he's probably pretty happy there. But maybe he wants to join a hot start-up, or maybe he's thinking about changing careers entirely. The potential change might not even be about work at all. Perhaps he needs time or flexibility to deal with a personal or family situation, or maybe circumstances are pushing him to relocate to a different area.

Can You Keep Him?

If your employee is looking to relocate or needs some flexibility beyond the regular nine-to-five workday, and you really like his work, here's your chance to become the coolest boss in the world: consider letting him relocate or change his schedule but continue to work for you. If his current position isn't a perfect fit, maybe you could tailor something similar that will work with his new situation. If he needs to relocate, it's quite possible that he hasn't found a job in the new location yet. Your offer could be a real lifesaver! As long as this worker is able to be fairly self-sufficient, he has proven to be productive, and the team can operate effectively with a remote member, then everyone wins.

I have successfully used this technique many times to retain excellent talent. Most of the time, things work out well. It is important, however, to monitor the situation closely. Occasionally, an employee's remote location can lead to problems—his individual productivity might decline, or the team's overall effectiveness could degrade. If that happens, you'll have to pull the plug and ask the employee to return or resign. At least you gave it a shot.

I'm So Proud of You!

On the other hand, it's pretty hard to argue with someone who's heading off to medical or law school. Be supportive, and work on a friendly exit. You could have a new doctor or lawyer in your future. Or he could decide that the career change wasn't for him after all and ask for his old job back.

The same is true if one of your workers is thinking of running off to join (or form) a hot start-up. Many higher-quality and younger employees will get this bug at some point. Chances are, he's looking at a completely different risk/reward equation than you're able to offer. If he isn't afraid to work sixty- or eighty-hour weeks, the possible rewards of doing so might far outweigh anything he now enjoys. Or if you *are* the hot start-up, maybe he's in a spot where he just needs the security and stability of a bigger, more established organization.

Be supportive! Granted, the start-up lifestyle is not for everyone. But I personally feel that those who never try it are missing out on a key life experience: the camaraderie, the readiness to change the world, the take-no-prisoners attack attitude, the excitement of solving problems, and the reward of gaining customers and approaching a lucrative endgame. The three years I spent at my first start-up were some of the most exhilarating of my entire career. I firmly believe that these are experiences everyone should have.

So feel excited for this person, wish him well, and offer to provide advice or feedback if he ever needs it. Most importantly, let him know that you'd welcome him back warmly should things go awry. He will very much appreciate the backstop, and he will respect you in a whole new way.

Being a Big Brother

But what if someone from your team is thinking about leaving for another local company—maybe one that's in a similar business as your own company? If he hasn't completely made up his mind (and assuming that you would rather keep him), you have the opportunity to help contribute to his decision. But how do you handle it gracefully? How do you help the employee do what's in his best interest, and not necessarily in your own?

First, use your practiced listening techniques to find out why your employee is attracted to the other company. Does he want a different type of work environment? Different types of projects? Greater compensation? The ability to work alongside past friends or closer to home? Listen carefully. Sometimes folks will say it's about money when it's really about something else, and sometimes they will say it's about something else when it's really about the money. When you're sure that all the cards are on the table, consider how you can actively respond to some of these points and develop a win-win solution for you both.

If the issue is compensation, and he is truly deserving, making a compensation adjustment can quickly bring the situation to a close. However, keep in mind that if this employee has gone so far as to actively seek a new position, any attempt to keep him may turn out to be only a temporary solution. If you offer more compensation, will that really solve all the issues at hand? If compensation really is the only complaint, how long will it be before he returns with the same issue? If a worker is worth his salt, someone out there will always pay more than you do. So before you let him go, ask yourself whether your employee is seeing the other good things that your company has to offer. The decision to leave needs to be made on much more than compensation alone, and salary is usually not the deciding factor in where someone chooses to work. That's why I encourage you to dig deeper when someone indicates that money is his primary issue.

If the real issue is about types of projects with which he's involved, that may be within your scope of control as well. What other tasks might he work on? Or if he's looking for a more flexible work environment, can you offer the option to telecommute a couple of days a week?

So, if you've gone this far, and he still isn't sure, what do you do? My approach here is to let my worker know, gently, that I understand that other options are available to him—the best people will always have other options. Then, I help him walk through whether this particular option is the right one for him. What is the other company's history? Are the products likely to be relevant for some time to come? Would he actually be working on the best products? What are the chances that the company might have to downsize? Does he know anything about the group with which he'll be working?

Keep in mind that you should ask these questions in the same way as his most trusted friend would. You want to be curious, not vicious.

It's okay for you to expose the more difficult truths about changing jobs, especially if he hasn't thought about them himself. There can be real danger involved in a move away from his existing position. With you, he's a top person on the totem pole. He's respected, well-known, and sought out for all the really big problems. On the other hand, as the newest worker at another company, still unproven, he'll be the most vulnerable in times of hardship. Be honest. But do not let him feel that you are trying to skew the facts to your advantage. As long as you approach the discussion factually and sensitively, he should appreciate your thoughts. And there's a good chance that after having such a supportive conversation, he'll think about sticking around after all.

But if he does finally decide to leave, leave the door open. If you chase him out of your office with a snarky "You're making a huge mistake! Don't call me when you figure that out," it will only validate his decision to go. And the word will spread that you are indeed a Dingus.

Moving Down the Hall

What if your valued employee is looking at another position within your company? Do not make the mistake of immediately trying to talk him out of it. Encourage him to look into it carefully, and welcome him to return for another discussion about what he finds. Always be supportive when an employee wishes to explore additional options, especially if it will keep the talent in the company family.

Once he's collected more information, lead him through the same kind of discussion we covered earlier to ensure that he's really thought through the positives and negatives. Help him come to the decision that's best for him.

Tuning Your Leadership to the Task

One of my favorite requests when I interview potential managers is this:

> "Pretend that you need a certain task done. You have decided to delegate it to one of your workers. You have called me, the lucky one, into your office to hand this task off to me. Tell me what you would say to convey this."

The typical response goes something like this:

> "I need you to do this task for me. Let's have a discussion about it so I can explain it to you and tell you why it's really important. Then I'll walk you through a good way to attack it. We can meet every day to discuss your progress."

The manager candidate thinks he has laid out a great plan. He will coach me very carefully. We'll be a team. He will not let me fail.

In reality, however, this potential manager—or any manager who responds this way!—has jumped to many conclusions without asking any questions. What if I have previous experience doing this task? What if I already know how important it is? Conversely, what if it isn't really important at all, but it needs to get done anyway? Might I learn more from this project if I am actually given the opportunity to fail at it?

For example, what if the candidate was a parent, I was a child, and the task was taking out the trash? Would we really need to have a discussion about why it's important? Would we need to walk through the process, given that I'd probably dumped the trash a million times already? Would we need progress updates? In this case, the only thing I need to know is that it's time to take out the trash.

Covering the Basics

Taking out the trash is a simple example. But maybe you're dealing with a simple task, or a complex one that the worker has already done many times. That's why you need to fine-tune every discussion like this, keeping in mind both the particular assignee and the task itself. You must account for the worker's past experience, his motivations, the overall effort the task requires, and many other factors. *Then* determine how to launch the worker into the task. Doing it the wrong way can lead to confusion, demotivation, resentment, and failure.

In general, your first determination should be whether the employee has ever done this type of task before. If you don't know, ask. If he has, you can go into much less detail on how to handle this particular instance. (How does it make you feel when someone explains how to do something you could do in your sleep?) Instead, just cover whatever factors might make this case a little different than usual, and let him know when you need it done. If necessary, give this person a couple of specific pointers or general guidelines for how you want it handled this time. Make plans to check in later if you need to provide feedback before it's complete. That's it. Send him off, and get on with your day.

But if your worker hasn't had the necessary experience with this task, you need to determine the best way to kick it off. And that can vary, depending on each individual's maturity level for the particular type of task. That level may vary for different tasks, but overall, most people tend to fall more or less into one of three general categories. I call them Tell, Sell, and Solo.

Tell

Some employees are perfectly happy to be told exactly what you want and exactly when, where, and how you want it done. They don't function well when a problem is delegated to them with no explanation or context. This doesn't make them bad workers—it simply means they respond best to direct instructions. And once they have them, they are anxious to get started. When you start explaining how important it is, though, you're just annoying them by keeping them longer. These are the Tell people.

Sell

Sell workers can be much like the Tells, but they have a hard time getting motivated to do the task unless they understand why it is important. They may know exactly how to handle the task, or you may need to lay out the method and process for them the same way you do for the Tells. But for the Sells, you need to cover the "why" part too. Otherwise, the motivation will be missing. If you don't make the case, progress will be slow or nil.

Solo

Unlike Tell and Sell workers, Solo workers would much rather devise their own paths to a solution. They may be fully capable of handling the entire problem when you delegate to them, or they might need you to participate with them to some degree on the Tell or Sell level. But for the most part they are capable of developing an appropriate solution on their own. They require a minimum of progress checking, and they have no desire for you to dictate to them how to do their job. Try it, and you will generate plenty of harsh feelings.

Getting It Done

Regardless of task maturity level, be sure to account for the individual's motivation in completing the task. This can be especially important for Sells, but it applies to everyone. If the task is exciting, you can worry a little less about having daily progress checks to make sure he's still working on the task, regardless of his maturity level or whether he's done it before or not. On the other hand, if it's grunt work, you're going to have to keep a closer eye on the situation—even for the Tells.

But while the task is under way, keep in mind that failure is not always a terrible thing. Depending on the particular circumstances, you may be able to afford a false start or two. No, you don't want to let someone waste weeks going off in the wrong direction with a project that should take a day or two. But what if the worker ends up discovering a completely different solution than you ever imagined? He could come back with a process for efficient cold fusion or solve world hunger, all while you thought he was going offtrack on that little job you gave him.

Even if that's unlikely, do give your people some slack to solve problems in their own ways when the task allows for it. They'll learn a lot in the process, and you'll learn more about how different people handle situations when you delegate to them. As you learn each person's task maturity level, you'll be able to use your knowledge to get them off to the best possible start on the next task, and you're bound to find more ways to mentor or coach them. If you do it right, over time you will watch your employees mature from Tell to Sell and eventually to some form of Solo. And ultimately you might end up with a better solution than you first thought possible. That is fun.

Continual Mentoring

One of your most important responsibilities as a manager is to guide all of your employees as they learn and grow. With technical and frontline workers, you will help them learn to do their jobs more efficiently, enhance their existing skills and gain new ones, move into more advanced positions, and generally grow to be more than they were when they first joined your team.

With managers, you have the same general responsibilities. But you also have an obligation to their subordinates and future employees: to make sure that none of your managers becomes a Dingus. Take every opportunity that presents itself to pass along the skills that you have learned for managing effectively. Teach your managers by example. And, of course, give them copies of this book!

As a good manager, take every opportunity you have to grow your employees. It's pretty straightforward to provide regular positive reinforcement and correction when needed. But if you keep an eye out for opportunities, you will also find many chances to grow your individual team members more casually, during your ordinary day-to-day interactions.

Let's talk about a couple of my favorite techniques for teaching employees better working skills—and how they can learn to better themselves.

Answering Questions with Questions

Imagine someone on your team asks you a question or comes to you with a problem he needs to solve. "Should I handle it like this or like that?" Maybe he thinks he knows the answer, but he wants to be sure that you will agree with him. Or maybe he really has no idea how to proceed. How should you respond?

Simple: *don't answer his question*. Anytime you're about to answer someone's question, remember that the best course of action is to merely ask the question right back to him. Hey, you're the boss! Enjoy the privilege!

But really, why the abstinence? It's just like when you're shutting up and actively listening—you want to find out what your worker is thinking and how he got there. No, you don't need to respond like this to "What time is the meeting?" But if you're going to help someone become more effective at solving problems, you can't just feed him the answer and hope he figures out why it was the right one. You need to make him propose the solution. And not just the solution—he needs to "show his work" by sharing the thought process that generated the solution. Getting your employee talking is the key to opening up (and then expanding) his brain.

So instead of answering the question directly, try something like "Well, what do you think we should do?" Psychologists have been successfully applying this method since the dawn of time. And no fair giving hints! As soon as you provide any sort of nudge toward the solution, you've biased him at best, and you may have lost what could have been a better answer than your own. If the employee continues with "I really just don't know," try changing your response to something like "Let's pretend I'm out of town and completely unreachable. What would you do?" He may realize what you're doing, but it will force him to take responsibility for the situation and come up with a plan.

Assessing the Solution

After you have prompted the worker to choose a course of action, assess it with him. Remember that you asked him to think aloud as he worked it out, so don't just check that his final answer is correct. Look at the assumptions that he used to make the decision and the path he took to reach it. If he happens to get the right answer simply by guessing, and you reply with nothing more than "Yes! Way to go!" and send him on his way, you really haven't provided any useful mentorship.

As you work through your employee's proposed solution, look for as many opportunities as possible to provide positive feedback. If he was perfectly correct every step of the way—the assumptions, the path to the solution, and the final answer—that's terrific! Even if he's chosen a completely incorrect course, there will probably be a few details that he gets right, and you should commend him for that. Either way, analyze the solution together, praise the strong points, and help him figure out where he made a misstep. If the employee simply hasn't had much experience in the area, you might need to provide some basic facts. In other cases, the facts will be correct already, and you'll need to work on nuances and more complicated assumptions. Just make sure you've done some good mentoring by the time the conversation finishes. With any luck, you'll leave the worker a little more "grown" than he was before the discussion.

Guiding Collaborative Solutions

An interesting corollary to the practice of prompting your people to reach their own solutions is when two (or more) of them come to you with something like "We can't agree on a solution to this problem."

Just like when you're working with a single employee, simply providing the answer they seek won't help them learn anything. Worse, an answer from On High that doesn't include any support other than "The boss wants it" will probably leave some members of the team less than committed to it.

So step back. Start by reminding your team that most work problems are composed of a set of truthful tidbits. Sure, people might have their own biases or emotions that can make it a little harder to be objective, but issues at work are rarely truly controversial. So start by guiding the team to set aside any emotion and focus on gathering the relevant facts. Once exposed, the data will point toward a solution that any reasonable team member should be able to accept—just like solving a mathematical equation.

Shutting Up

Much of the time, this is enough to enable your group to go on and solve the dilemma themselves, though you may need another round or two of impartial mentoring and questioning to get them over the finish line.

Why does this work? In a group environment, a high-functioning team can feed off each other and use their group expertise to come to a better solution than any individual team member could reach on his own. And when you ask your team to reach a decision themselves, you'll find that every team member will buy into the eventual solution—because every team member will have examined and understood the steps that were required to get there. (Remember the Sells? This is how they will learn to sell themselves and each other!)

Of course, there will almost certainly be some times when you will need to insert yourself into the decision-making process and make a final call, just as the Vice President sometimes needs to cast a tie-breaking vote in the Senate. Valid differences of opinion do exist, and sometimes they need to be handled by a third party. One Dingus boss I knew felt that there was never a reason for two of his managers to come to him with a disagreement. His reply was always a screamed "You should be able to figure this out yourselves!" It was a disaster. Simple problems would arise between departments and begin working themselves up the food chain, and when they reached the level of this Dingus's direct reports, they hit a wall. If the two managers couldn't agree on a solution, nothing got done about it. Ever. This led to a festering mass of rancid pork where there once had been a functioning organization. It also led to the Dingus's eventual forced retirement.

So be prepared to step in and make a call when you need to—that's another part of being the boss. But take that step only as a last resort. And when you do, remember that the solution will not coincide with every person's initial position. Go the extra mile to get commitment from everyone involved that they will support the decision and not undermine it. (We'll talk about that shared commitment more in the "Getting Respect" chapter.)

Communicating with Peers

Many of the techniques that we have already discussed are easily applicable to communication with your peers and superiors, as well as your subordinates. Let's discuss a couple more tips that will enhance your positive relationships with other leaders.

The Run-It-By

You just finished writing a document, creating a process, or designing a reorganization. You're probably getting ready to go to the team members that it will affect and start getting their feedback.

Wait! The people who work for you will probably have some good ideas to help you improve what you've done, but before you speak with them, ask yourself whether any of your peers might be able to help too. Maybe one of them has done something similar and can give you some insight derived from his own experience. Maybe the simple fact that he's in roughly the same position that you are will allow him to catch something important in context that you happened to overlook. Or maybe it's all new to him. But even if it is, the very act of doing a quick "run-it-by" says that you care about what he thinks. If you gain nothing else from the conversation, you'll definitely have enhanced your relationship with one of your peers. And you're also more likely to see the favor returned when a fellow manager is planning some action that could have a trickle down (or trickle-over) effect on your own team.

Please note that this works even in cases where the other manager works in a completely different area and has no idea of the context in which you're working. He still has a team of his own, and a great deal of leadership skill can apply regardless of the area under his management.

"How Am I Doing?"

Besides your boss and your workers, your peers are another great place to look for feedback on your own performance. Because you're not a superior or a subordinate, they might not think to mention it if it isn't a pressing issue. But chances are, they have some useful observations they could share.

So make it a habit to sit down in a fellow manager's office every few months and ask something like "How am I doing here?" Encourage him to tell you what he's observed of your performance and share anything he's gathered from his own team. And then shut up and listen! He could have some genuinely helpful feedback on something you did poorly, in which case you can improve yourself at the same time as you build your relationship with him. Or if he got some bad information about you (or any part of your team) through the rumor mill, you can discuss the real situation with him. He will appreciate the fact that you value his feedback, and once again you'll have worked to build a closer relationship.

Communicating Upward, Summing Up, and Moving On

Just to round out the topic of one-on-one communication, there's one other person with whom it's crucial to have good communication: your boss (or bosses, if you're unlucky enough to be stuck in an *Office Space* situation with more than one). This topic is covered in the "Managing the Boss" chapter later in the book.

To sum up: when you begin a one-on-one talk with someone, and during the conversation, it's important to pay close attention. While you listen, actively think to yourself:

- What does this conversation really seem to be about?
- What is below the surface here? Is there something driving this talk that I need to uncover?
- What style should I be using to handle this type of conversation?
- Does my history with this person suggest I might need to alter my style a little?
- How can I learn from this talk? How can I help the other party learn or improve himself?
- Am I doing too much talking? (Sometimes, right in the middle of a chat with someone, I'll suddenly realize that I'm doing exactly that. I'll immediately start shutting up and listening, taking care to ask clarifying questions and let the other person talk.)

Now that we have discussed myriad types of individual interactions, let's expand our horizons and optimize the process of …

Chapter 3:
Communicating with the Group

When you're interacting with two or more people at the same time, many of the one-on-one communication techniques we've discussed are still valuable. Never overlook the opportunity to mentor your people, whether it's one at a time or all of them at once. But working with a group is often more of a teamwork thing than a mentoring thing, and there are a number of new factors that come into play when it happens. This chapter will focus on those.

Let's start our discussion with techniques to use in those omnipresent time-tested messes we call ...

Meetings

I could write a book about the problems with unnecessary, unproductive, and otherwise useless meetings, and I bet you could too. So let's just agree to sidestep the more general concepts of meeting (in)efficiency here. Instead, let's focus on a few key points for you, the leader, to keep in mind so you can avoid being the meeting's Dingus. (This discussion will focus only on planning and status meetings with a small group of your subordinates.

Presentations and departmental meetings with your entire team, or multiple teams, are discussed later in this chapter.)

In the "Continual Mentoring" section in the previous chapter, I shared some techniques for dealing with a couple of folks who have come to you to solve their problem for them. Those same points are totally applicable to meetings in general. Most importantly, do not go into a meeting with the attitude that you own it. You are going to *lead* it, but if your plan is to dominate it, and ultimately deliver it to some predetermined goal or solution, you've already failed. Your team will quickly learn how it goes when you're in charge. If they bother to show up at all, they will have gone out of their way to not prepare anything of value for it. Why bother, if you're going to show up and tell them exactly what's what anyway?

What your meeting *does* need is a good facilitator. In fact, this is so important that some companies hire or appoint dedicated facilitators. To me, however, taking that step is a sign of broken internal leadership. A balanced, participative, inclusive manager should be able to handle the leadership function.

And what does a good meeting leader do? You help get the meeting off on the right foot. You help steer it gently back on track when it strays. You make sure everyone's input is sought, and that the meeting isn't taken over by one or two of the more assertive attendees. You make sure that all participants support the outcome. And when it's appropriate, you gently add your own ideas to the meeting.

Sending the Invitation

A good leader can set a meeting up for success—or failure—before the meeting even begins. It starts when you send the invitation. If you want to be Mr. Dingus, be sure to use a cryptic title, provide no agenda or goals, schedule the meeting to span about six hours, invite ten different people who have little or no need to attend, and omit a couple of key people while you're at it. That oughta do it.

Or, you could do the opposite and give your meeting a fighting chance of success.

The Topic and Agenda

Seriously, you don't need to go overboard with the invitation title. But be specific enough: "Product Planning" or "Problem Discussion" doesn't quite do the trick, but "Review March Milestones for Project X" or "Discuss Reducing Travel Costs" does. Simply giving your meeting a good title will get people thinking about the topic before they get there.

As for the agenda, don't try to timebox every part of the meeting. But something like this will help significantly:

> "Please come prepared with your best three ideas for reducing our travel costs (no matter how outlandish). We will combine our ideas, brainstorm, and rank order to arrive at the best possibilities. Arrive on time."

When you specify a clear title and agenda, people will arrive prepared and ready to go. They will understand how far you expect the meeting to go. In the example above, it's clear that you are planning to expose possibilities, but you aren't intending to fully implement solutions. Your agenda is to gather ideas and sort them into the best choices going forward.

Who to Invite

Everyone hates being stuck in meetings where they aren't needed. But it's almost as bad to be left out of something that you really need to know about. As you make up the attendee list, consider the old joke about "chickens" and "pigs": when you serve up a tasty breakfast of bacon and eggs, the chicken is *involved* or *interested*, but the pig is *committed*.

Now, look at each invitee and determine whether he is a chicken or a pig. Usually, most of your pigs should be there. Sometimes one pig is fully capable of representing the others, though, and if you know that to truly be the case, keep the attendance down. Chickens, on the other hand, should be excluded by default unless you feel that one or two of them might have genuine expertise or something positive to add to the discussion.

If you're undecided, you can easily identify a chicken in the room by looking to see who is checking email on his iPad. Chickens can always get a postmortem debrief or read the minutes. Keep the invite list as small as possible, and your meetings will run far more efficiently.

By the way, don't forget to consider your own chicken or pig status either. If you are a chicken, maybe the topic's Chief Pig should be there in your place!

Keep It Quick

How long should the meeting be? I hate meetings in general, and I firmly believe that most stuff we formalize in them can be handled as quick hallway discussions. Plus, the more time your team spends in meetings, the less they're really getting done.

So keep it as quick as you can. In some organizations, I have actually *removed the chairs from the conference room* to train my people to get to the meat of the matter quickly. They may have grumbled, but it sure cut down on a lot of wasted time and circular arguments.

If you don't want to go that far, use hour-long meetings as your default. Except for when you're working on particularly large issues, one hour should be plenty of time to achieve your goals. And if an hour isn't enough, consider splitting the overall meeting up into a few hour-long chunks. Most people have a hard time concentrating on a single issue for more than an hour anyway. After that, the ever-present tug of all those other things they have to get done makes it difficult to maintain focus. (Be honest. What's your first thought when someone schedules an all-freaking-day meeting for *you*? Yeah, exactly.) But within that one-hour window, you should have every expectation that a well-focused meeting will command each person's full attention for the duration.

What about shorter meetings—those you expect to go fifteen minutes or half an hour? Generally, I like to schedule generously. If fifteen minutes turns into twenty because something unusual pops up, but you have thirty minutes on the calendar, the overrun won't mess up the rest of the day. And if you expect to finish a discussion in thirty minutes, it rarely hurts to schedule a full hour. If you underestimate the task at hand, the extra time means you still stand a good chance of getting things wrapped up without having to cram in another meeting later in the day. And if you finish early, everyone will love having that time back in their day—*their* time, because your meeting had blocked it out on the calendar. You will be a fan favorite.

While I'm at it, here are a few more scheduling tips:

- When I say, "Schedule the meeting for an hour," what I really mean is "Schedule the meeting for fifty-five minutes." Leave those five minutes at the end to allow everyone to get to the next meeting on time. It respects the leader of the next meeting, and when that meeting does start on time, it makes the meeting that much more likely to achieve its goals.
- If you use Google Calendar, open the settings and find the

Default Meeting Length area. Enable the Speedy Meetings option to cut meetings off a little early. Use it!

- Recommend to your team that they set their calendar alerts to remind them five minutes before a meeting begins. (Most email programs use a default of fifteen minutes.) When a fifteen-minute alert goes off, and you're still in the middle of the previous meeting, everyone just ignores the reminder. And if you're at your desk, working, you're really going to ignore it. But if the alert pops up just five minutes in advance, there's no doubt about it—it's time to go.

Is a Recurrent Meeting Needed?

Take a look at the meetings you have scheduled now. How many do you have at regularly scheduled intervals? It's a good bet that many of them shouldn't be. Oftentimes people show up for a regular meeting by default, only to find that there is a minimal or nonexistent agenda. Then they stop showing up at all, or the meeting arranger simply keeps canceling it. Look at your recurring meetings and consider whether a longer interval between meetings might be appropriate, or even if calling the meeting only on demand would be a better use of everyone's time.

Running the Meeting

Once you're in the meeting itself, there are several things you can do to get the most out of the time that the group is together.

Start On Time

Remember my request to "arrive on time" in the sample agenda above? I use that reminder for a reason. Although people tend to get accustomed to that and read over it, they won't ignore it for long when you lock the conference room door three minutes after the meeting's start time. You might sacrifice a little productivity by excluding someone (or a few someones) the first time you do it, but it won't happen too often after that. In fact, in the invitation, you might as well put, "Arrive on time. Door will be locked three minutes in."

Even if you don't go that far, do start on time whether everyone is ready or not. They'll figure it out. Otherwise, people will quickly learn that your 9:00 meeting never starts until 9:05 ... or 9:10 ... or whenever everyone actually decides to show up. Choose a start time and stick to it.

And, if possible, it's a good idea to avoid being late to your own meetings.

Keep the Focus

During the meeting, you need to strike a balance between unnecessary rigidity and total free-for-all. You want to keep it on track, without suppressing contributions from everyone else.

First, stay alert for indications that the meeting is beginning to divert off its productive course. Use the agenda from your initial meeting invitation as a guide. If your goal is only to brainstorm ideas, and people begin discussing how to implement those solutions, it's time to steer the conversation back to where it's supposed to be. Do so gently, at least the first time or two that it strays:

> "Hey, everyone, it sounds like you have some pretty good ideas about how we would proceed with this. But let's finish getting all the ideas out first, okay?"

Another tip-off that things are starting to stray is when people begin having multiple, separate conversations. Chances are that at least one of those side discussions is off the primary path—and even if they're all on topic, some people are missing what others are saying. You want to limit multiple simultaneous discussions anyway, but you especially need to discontinue the ones that detract from the central goal of the meeting.

Finally, keep an eye out for the appearance of a smartphone or prolonged attention to a tablet or laptop. When people start checking email in the middle of the meeting, it's another great sign that they're losing interest—quite possibly because things are wandering offtrack.

Stay Away from Email!

Speaking of checking email during a meeting, there's a one-word rule for this: *don't*.

If you're paying attention to the tips I've already laid out about chickens and pigs, keeping it short, limiting recurring meetings, and so on, that means the meetings you do attend are usually pretty important. And yet you can't give the topic an hour of your uninterrupted attention? If you have the habit of pulling out your phone to check email during meetings, there's no better way to send a wonderful message to your team that whatever else is going on is far more important than what you're supposed to be working on together. Stop it right now. The same goes for the rest of your team.

I'm not saying you need to turn off or confiscate everyone's phone at the start of the meeting. Emergencies happen. But there are very few legitimate reasons that phones should come popping out of their holsters during the discussion.

Going past smartphones, what about laptops and tablets? Do you bring yours to meetings? There are only two reasons for that: if you're sharing a presentation or legitimately using it to take meeting minutes. Otherwise, the presence of your laptop is nothing more than a distraction. The same goes for everyone else in the meeting. Make the rule and follow it.

While I'm ranting, let me channel Jerry Seinfeld for a minute and do another one. "What's the deal with email notifications on your phone?" Given that you most likely get a few emails every hour of the workday, what's the point of turning on a vibrating notification for new messages? (Heaven help you if you use an audible notification!) If you last checked for email fifteen minutes ago, what are the odds that a new message will be there if you check again right now? Inevitably, the answer is "almost certainly." So why do you need the alert? Yeah, there's an email waiting for you … all the freaking time. Surprise.

Make it easy: turn email notifications off. If it's that important, they will call you.

Participating as a Contributor Instead of The Boss

When you're leading a meeting, it can be a fine balancing act to get your own points considered without inadvertently shutting down a lot of ideas from the other members of your team. And even when someone else is handling the meeting-management duties, you're still the boss, and many people will have a natural instinct to defer to you. So whether or not you're in charge of a meeting, if you don't handle yourself carefully, you will find that your ideas are somehow always deemed "the best." You need to make sure that you're gathering the *real* best ideas, even when they aren't yours.

To help you counteract the possibility of losing those best ideas, let's return to some of the communication points we've already discussed. Many of the same techniques we discussed for one-on-one dialogues and mentoring opportunities will apply just as well when you're meeting with a group. Most importantly, you must enter the meeting without a bias toward any particular solution—especially if it's originally yours. There's no point in asking your team to be part of a dialogue that's really a monologue! So be prepared to shut up and listen to the group the same way you communicate one-on-one: listen far more than you speak, help summarize points as they're made, and actively acknowledge great ideas as they're mentioned.

Ask Open Questions

If you ask questions, be sure to phrase them in an "open" way that doesn't give away your own personal bias. "Should we do plan A or plan B?" will create a much more open atmosphere for discussion than "Don't you think we should do plan A?" or "Is anyone stupid enough to think that plan B is better?"

And just as you would watch and listen for underlying questions and issues when you're speaking with an individual, pay attention to what the group isn't saying. That quiet person in the corner may be the smartest employee you have, but he could be nervous about opening his mouth in the middle of a big group. If you think someone could have a valid perspective to add, draw him out with open questions like "What do you think of plan A versus plan B?"

Ask Closed Questions

Not that there's never a right time for a "closed" question. Here's a fun party trick that you should pull out of your bag at least once. When you feel that the group is getting close to choosing a course of action, or if you really need to get everyone moving in the same direction, and you agree with the logic behind the approaching course, try asking a "closed" question that goes in exactly the opposite direction. For example, if most of the team is homing in on plan A, and it seems like the right plan to you as well, try something like "I'm really thinking that plan B looks good, though, don't you?"

There are a couple of things that can happen now. Ideally, everyone will jump up with explanations of why plan B is a bad idea. If that happens, you have to be willing to look a tiny bit ignorant to keep the discussion alive, but you can eventually agree with the counterarguments and move the decision along. Eventually, many of your folks will learn to recognize this tactic, but even when they know you're playing Devil's Advocate it will continue to work.

On the other hand, the Devil's Advocate approach is a great way to identify whether you have any yes-men in the group. They will most likely start to do 180s to support your stated position, even though you know that it isn't really supported by the facts.

It's always good to know who your yes-men are. They can be good contributors, but if they always agree with you, you can't necessarily trust them to represent factual positions that counter your own. Over time, however, a good manager will build up trust with these individuals. You'll let them see that disagreeing with you isn't a résumé-generating event (as one of my recent leaders liked to call it). But that trust will only come when they see you actively support respectful disagreement, listen to counterarguments with an open mind, and modulate your own positions when good facts and well-formed arguments warrant it.

Be Positive and Supportive

Have you ever noticed the strange predisposition we all seem to have toward negative language, even when we're not really feeling negative at all? This is particularly noticeable in meetings where someone's response to an idea or comment begins with the word "no," even though the responder is actually agreeing with the comment.

Member 1: "I have looked at all the facts, and I think it's totally possible for us to get that done as planned, if we implement this other change. What do you think?"

Member 2: "No, I agree."

I know this seems like a silly example, but listen for it in real life. It happens way more often than you might expect. I started hearing it about twenty years ago, and I still hear it today. When I point this out to people, they are often completely surprised to realize they'd been doing it. But once they knew, they started hearing it more around them too.

Sometimes the "no" is more like "yeah, no" or "no, yeah," but it happens. The second person is in agreement with the first one, but he still frames the reply as a disagreement. Although the injection of the "no" may not seem like much, it can send subconscious signals that the previous comments were not useful or less than correct. Even if you think it does no real harm, why not go out of your way to start with "yeah" instead?

Plus, when someone makes a good point and you have another point to follow up, acknowledge the previous comment first. "Yeah, that's a great idea. Something else I was thinking about is …" It seems simple. But every time you take the opportunity to make someone feel a little better about what he has to offer, he will be more willing to repeat that behavior. Over time, that's going to lead to a lot of great ideas that otherwise may never have come out.

Getting Support Without a Consensus

So when is it okay to do a little dictating?

Sometimes, meetings are not intended to seek a consensus solution. You may have a specific need to force a decision in a particular direction, and the meeting is more about announcing it and gathering support. That can happen, especially when you have knowledge that you are not permitted to share that has major bearing on your own team's direction—like an upcoming reorganization or acquisition—but you've been put under the cloak of silence. In situations like that, you must make it perfectly clear at the start of the meeting that the group is not there to decide on a course of action. Let your team know that you appreciate that others might have something else to suggest, but the direction is already locked and loaded. If you are able to share the background information, great! If not, simply say, "I have some information relevant to our discussion, but I'm not permitted to share it."

If you think your team will disown you if you admit that you can't share something, think again. If you treat your team well, they'll generally be reasonable. Your team understands that they can't be privy to every bit of knowledge you might have, especially about things that are larger than the team itself. Own up to it. Then, let your team know that their participation is still important to the big picture, and that you're counting on their support.

And besides, what other choice do you have? If you push in a certain direction without admitting your motives, the team will pick up on that and realize you have some kind of hidden agenda. And I don't think we need to discuss what will happen if you divulge the underlying confidential information.

There's also a middle ground here. Sometimes there's plenty of room for the team to contribute toward a solution, but for some reason you aren't going to require a consensus or agreement at the end of the discussion. Again, maybe you have secret information, or maybe it's just a situation where you have many more years of experience and have already charted the correct course. In this case, let the team know that their contributions are necessary and welcome, and that you may not have your mind made up yet. But be clear that when all is said and done, the decision is going to be yours to make. Think of this as a consultative meeting. You're consulting the team and gathering feedback, but the final call is up to you.

Leaving with One Voice

No matter what type of meeting you're having, it's important that all participants go forth and act on the meeting's solution as if it was their own idea from the beginning. If the meeting was designed to reach a consensus decision, that shouldn't be too difficult—the very intent of the meeting suggests that everyone needs to buy in. However, after a consultative meeting, there can certainly be people who disagree strongly with your decision. That in itself is a good reason to avoid the practice when feasible—you don't want your people thinking, *Yeah, the boss listened to my logic and ignored it*. Not the makings of a loyal following. This only gets worse if you've had to basically dictate a decision or make an announcement without requesting input from others. Regardless of how you arrived at the final decision, however, everyone in the meeting should verbally confirm their intended compliance with the "I will fully support this decision as if it was my own" mantra.

If the group was composed of only frontline workers, that isn't always easy, but it's pretty straightforward. But when it's managers on your staff that have to support and implement the given solution, it can be a lot tougher. You're asking them to sign off on a decision when they don't buy into it, and furthermore you're asking them to go out and get all of their people in line with it too. Situations like these can be great opportunities for you to further mentor your managers, particularly if you've had experience as the one who's being expected to support an unpopular decision made by your own manager. Supporting your boss is a critical skill, worthy of much more discussion on its own. We'll get to it in the "Getting Respect" chapter later on.

Just Stop Already!

Finally, one more thing about meetings in general. It's my simple, basic mantra: Just stop already!

In this section, we've discussed a lot of ways to better handle your meetings. But a lot of it boils down to simply *not having them* (or not attending) if you don't have to. And the same should go for your people. Demonstrate by having as few of your own meetings as possible, and encourage your team members who lead meetings themselves to look for every opportunity to sidestep the formal sit-down. Then ask your workers to scrutinize each meeting invitation carefully when it arrives. Does he really need to be there? Will he be a chicken or a pig? Would a review of the meeting minutes or a quick summary from the meeting leader be enough? If your people are managers, will their presence in a meeting slant it somehow in a negative way? Even if not, would it be a waste of their time to attend?

Remember that every minute you spend in a meeting is time that you are not spending one-on-one with the members of your team. That's true for your managers too. If you need to prevent other people from overloading your calendar, try blocking out a couple of hours each day that no one can book. Even better, set a personal limit of half your workday as the maximum amount of time you're willing to spend in meetings. If you currently spend nearly your entire day in meetings, this will seem unfathomable to you at first. Just try it.

If you follow the tips here and pick and choose carefully, you will still be involved in all the meetings for which you really need to be present. But you will find yourself with a mass of newfound useful time. That's time to spend interacting, mostly one-on-one, with your employees. They will appreciate it greatly. And you'll probably have more time to communicate with your own boss, which can't hurt either.

Later, we will discuss a technique for dropping in on meetings (when you truly would be a chicken) for the purpose of "just seeing what's going on." This requires careful balance, and it can only be accomplished after your folks have learned about the technique and understand that it is not a threat to them.

Email Communication

Here is a simple fact: email sucks for real communication.

Of course email has its place! Use it for straightforward announcements, minor requests, and other items of a simple, factual nature. "The meeting will be at 2 PM." Or "Can you send me a copy of the TPS report?"

But as soon as you try to use email for anything complicated, you are asking for trouble. "Can you tackle this project for me?" Or "How come you did that?" Think again! Do not relegate anything that could be considered controversial, in any way whatsoever, to the emotional black hole of an expressionless email. And no, adding that cute little smiley face doesn't help. Seriously. The very fact that you have to use a smiley face in an attempt to clarify your emotions is proof that the written word is not enough to communicate everything you intend. And, worse, you can't see the recipient's reaction as it's happening, either.

There is no excuse to carry on an important "conversation" over email. If you can't physically walk over and talk with your employee, pick up the phone. Launch Skype or FaceTime. Anything. Just don't start typing.

And why would you want to? A good manager relishes every opportunity to work face-to-face with everyone on the team. That kind of contact prevents miscommunications and allows you to tailor your talking points dynamically, insert emotion as needed, and adjust the whole experience to how the employee is reacting. Working face-to-face allows you to shut up, listen, and learn at the same time you're teaching. It is one of the simplest things you can do to avoid becoming a Dingus.

What if one of your employees (or anyone, for that matter) emails something inappropriate to you? I don't mean anything legally or morally questionable—I mean any subject that doesn't lend itself well to an email discussion. Improve the situation immediately by picking up your feet instead of responding with a reply email. Pick up the phone if you must. But do not click the Reply button.

Make sure that your employees follow the same rules with each other as well. You will promote far more productive team dynamics and probably avoid a few flame wars along the way. Or course, every once in a while someone will still send the dreaded flame message or start a very controversial discussion with an email addressed to about twenty names. That offender ends up in my office for a brain cleansing. Does he really think that email is the most efficient way to discuss and settle something that contentious? Fix it quickly, and everyone will be better off.

Presenting to the Team

Many books delve deeply into public speaking. It's an art that is improved and perfected only with great practice. The basic concepts—getting over your nervousness by visualizing the audience in only their underwear, for example—can be gleaned from other sources at your leisure. Therefore, I am not going to talk much about presenting to an auditorium full of people.

The message here is about speaking in front of your team. When you stand in front of your employees to deliver a message, you have the opportunity to develop a deeper rapport with them as they see you in action. If you handle it well, many of the team members will come away feeling like you connected with them personally, almost as if you had just finished a one-on-one sit-down with them. By sharing your message in group mode, you can accomplish this with dozens or even hundreds of people at once. There's a great return on investment!

Be Positively Honest

For obvious reasons, there is a lot of overlap between leading a meeting and presenting a message. Let me start with the single, most important rule you can follow, one that really applies to every part of your job: Be as honest as possible.

Sounds easy enough, doesn't it? Unfortunately, true honesty is often much more difficult than it first appears. There are many difficult topics that can tempt you to wander around the truth: upcoming raises (or the lack thereof), the status of an ailing product in the field, slow progress on a new development, or the prospect of major negative actions like downsizing or salary reductions. Unfortunately, sometimes such hedging is truly unavoidable, and I'll talk about it a little more in the "Dealing with Confidential Information" section later. But those situations are rare.

Most of the time, however, your presentation will be more along the lines of an all-team progress report. If everything is going well, good for you! But sometimes things are more awkward. If a project is veering off course, and it's starting to feel a little embarrassing, would it be okay to skip lightly over some of the more negative items and just focus on the positive ones?

Sadly, no. In fact, I can assure you that this is an awful idea. Your people can smell dishonesty as easily as a dog smells fear. Among them, everyone in the room knows pretty much everything that's going on anyway—you're mostly there to sum it all up at once. And if you start omitting relevant facts to make things seem overtly better than they really are, it won't take long for the team to realize it. And there goes your credibility.

That doesn't mean that you can be nasty and pinpoint blame, even if you could truthfully place it on a few individuals. But you can certainly say things like "We've had a few unexpected detours on the XYZ project. Unfortunately, it's now looking to come in two or three weeks later than we scheduled." Some people in your audience already know that it's true, so you might as well discuss it.

The important point here is how you *follow* that statement. This is your grand opportunity to balance the negative points with how you intend to get things moving in a positive direction again. Things go wrong—that's life. But when you can follow up "The project is coming in late" with "We're putting two more people on it" or "We're going to remove the extra reporting feature, which will save us a week," it demonstrates active, positive leadership that will set the boat on course again. And everyone will feel like insiders into both the problem and the intended solution.

Hedging Your Bets

At other times, issues arise that you can openly discuss, but there's a different reason you need to hedge—you don't have definitive answers for everything yet. It is still important to have that discussion. Instead of leaving everyone wondering what the heck is going on, expose the thought processes that are under way, and share what you know about the various possible outcomes. Here's an example from the real world:

> "Folks, this is Captain Joe up in the cockpit. We can't push back yet because something's wrong with one of the engines, and we're bringing the mechanics out to take a look at it. Hopefully, they'll figure it out quickly, and we hope this won't take more than a few minutes."

Captain Joe has no idea how long this is going to take, and he's trying to let you down gently. But is that really the best course of action? If you catch yourself about to use the word *hope*, rethink it. Of course Captain Joe is *hoping*, but what does he know that is *factual*?

If you're going to convey iffy information, use words like "possibly," "probably," "unlikely," or "almost certainly" instead of the nebulous "hope." These words transmit the true thought process on your part, and they help give everyone a reasonable expectation of what's to come. Don't hesitate to toss in "Please don't hold me to this!" if necessary. The honest assessment of the situation is what's important, and it helps everyone feel like you're all in it together.

See how I said "honest assessment" there? That's another key. Just as you need to be honest when you're delivering a message that isn't totally comfortable, you need to be honest about the potential outcomes of an ongoing situation. When you're not sure how something is going to go, resist the temptation to slant your words to give your listeners the impression that the best possible outcome is likely. I'm not saying that you need to lean toward the worst possible outcome, either. But you need to be realistic. Odds are that you'll end up with something less than the best possible outcome.

When the situation does resolve itself, it's human nature that people will be more or less pleased *with the same outcome* depending on how you slanted their expectations. If you lead people to believe that that best outcome is very likely, and it doesn't happen, they're going to be less pleased than if you had given them a more realistic expectation in advance. But if you've prepped them for a relatively bad outcome, and something better happens, they'll be pleasantly surprised. I know that might be like putting whipped cream on a scoop of mud, but it can still have a positive effect.

Case in point: If Captain Joe feels that the delay will be in the thirty- to sixty-minute range, but he tells you that it's going to be only a few minutes, you might not be bothered at first. But when those thirty-plus minutes drag out, it's going to lead to cussing. On the other hand, if the captain comes out and says that the delay could be as much as an hour or two, and it turns out to be only forty-five minutes, you're going to be thrilled.

Dealing with Confidential Information

Earlier, I mentioned the dilemma that can arise when you're working around a scenario in which you can (or must) share some information about a current situation that's brewing or a change you're implementing, but you aren't at liberty to discuss all of the specifics of the situation or the reasons behind your decision. As I said then, it's okay to acknowledge that something is going on but that you aren't permitted to talk about it. Your team will understand that you are simply not in a position to discuss it yet. But do let them know that you'll be sure to fill them in as soon as you're able.

But what if something is brewing that your team is not supposed to know about? You know the possibilities: downsizing, a possible acquisition, a pending business deal. Unfortunately, rumors happen. So what if someone asks, "Is there any truth to the rumor that the company will be laying some people off?" (He may not ask the question in a group meeting; confidentiality applies equally to one-on-one conversations.) Assuming that upper management is not yet ready to release any word about the pending change, you have no choice but to cover these situations with a response like "I know of no plans for that at this time." You have to use that response whether or not layoffs are coming, or even whether layoff discussions are happening at all. Even if it's good news, like a huge new contract, if it's confidential, it's confidential. Period.

In the case of bad news, this is one of the sad times to be a manager. But what else can you really do? You're not permitted to allow people to know it's under consideration. So the most important thing you can do is *be consistent* about what you say and how you say it. If you try to be a little more honest by tweaking your response based on whether you really do have any knowledge, your team will eventually be able to compare your history of responses to what actually played out. Then they'll be able to translate the way you respond to future issues. You cannot allow that to happen.

At the end of the day, remember that you never want to give your folks any ammunition to brand you as untrustworthy in your communications. With the exception of those no-win scenarios, honesty really is the best policy. Stick to these guidelines, and your people will come to know they can rely on what you've said and trust you to communicate honestly. And once you gain their trust, they'll reward you with more open communication on their side as well.

Wrapping It Up

Finally, at the end of every presentation, be sure to leave some time for Q&A. You probably won't get many questions, but there are always a couple of people in any group who are willing to take the chance. And over time, more people will learn from experience that asking questions, even tough ones, isn't grounds for dismissal.

You should also feel free to "plant" a question or two in advance. If someone comes to you with a good question a few days before the presentation, ask him to please ask it again after you speak. (Of course, you don't have to leave him hanging until then! You can answer the question privately right away.)

Make sure to allow time for people to ask questions, and not just for you to answer them. I am always amazed by how little time some presenters allow between "Are there any questions?" and "Okay, bye!" The average is about two seconds. That is far short of the time needed for someone to decide that:

- He has a question.
- It won't look like a stupid question.
- It probably wasn't answered while he was dozing off.
- Asking it won't get him in trouble.
- It won't annoy the rest of the team by keeping them there longer.

Here's another great time to invoke the Seven Mississippi rule. More often than not, someone will take the bait and ask a solid question. And after you answer, do Seven Mississippi again. Give your people every opportunity to communicate, and communicate they will.

Miscellaneous Tips

Here are a few other, completely random items and suggestions for public speaking and presentations that I've learned over the years.

- Use minimal words on your slides—bullet points are great—and talk to your points. If anyone else could deliver your presentation for you simply by reading your slides out loud, or if you deliver it by reading your slides, you've screwed up. Your audience will be so transfixed by reading your slides that they'll miss anything else you have to say. You'll also look much less knowledgeable about your subject matter.

- Check over your presentation before you deliver it, and remove anything that's extraneous to your key point. Don't confuse your audience by trying to deliver two messages at once. If you do intend to deliver multiple messages, make the delineation between them clear and summarize one message before moving on to the next one.

- Rehearse your talk for timing, and then assume it will take twice as long when you actually give it. Extra words always seem to find their way in when you go live. You also need to leave more time if you expect to be taking questions during your talk.

- Try not to talk in hyperbole. When everything is "absolutely the best" or "totally the worst," you tend to lose impact. Stay balanced. (This actually applies to all of your communications, not only when addressing a group.)

- When you try to rush your talk, it only makes it take longer. Worse, you will lose your audience. If you've got too much to go over in the time allotted, scale back.

- Your jokes will never go over as well as you think they will. Choose them carefully. One of the best comments I ever heard was from a recent boss. He related a story that should have resulted in laughter, but it bombed. His follow-up was "And the reason I brought that up was because it was much funnier in rehearsal!" That brought the house down!

Departmental Meetings

Take a look at almost any company-wide survey asking for general employee feedback on what's working well and what's not. Almost invariably, "communication" will top the "not so good" list. Even if the communications are pretty good, they're still not good enough. Workers tend to feel left out of the loop quite easily. (Though I must admit to having once seen the comment "There are too many communications!")

The vacuum tends to form in the time frame of two to four weeks. You may have thoroughly communicated everything that was going on a few weeks ago, but after those few weeks have gone by, your team will start to feel like they are out of touch. You need to make them feel like they're always in the loop.

At the very least, schedule a departmental briefing every month for everyone who reports to you, either directly or indirectly. If you hold the meeting monthly, concentrate on important items, keep up the pace, and layer in a little humor, you should be able to provide enough information to get everyone back into the loop in no more than thirty to sixty minutes.

The good news is that this is actually a great opportunity for you to do much more than speak—you can also get everybody rowing the boat in unison. My experience has shown that a message must be communicated two to three times before everybody really hears it, and five to ten times before they start believing it. Take advantage of these prescheduled opportunities, and your bigger messages will start sinking in that much sooner. Of course, the presentation tips in the previous section will also help you get your message across even more successfully.

Use Special Presenters

Your monthly meeting is a great time to bring in special presenters from within your team. No need to do the whole thing yourself! Not only does a new voice offer the gathering a more dynamic feel, it also gives others an opportunity to address the team. Choose someone with unique knowledge, or someone who'd like to show off something particularly interesting that he's been working on.

Of course, the first time you allow someone new to present like this, it is critical that you dry-run his talk with you ahead of time. All too often, a newbie will go way over the allotted time or forget to focus on the salient points of his talk. If you train a few regular presenters, however, you'll eventually be able to trust that they understand what's required with no dry run needed.

Keep Going through the Crunch

I've known some managers to use frequent departmental meetings quite well, only to abandon them when projects were into their final stages and time was getting precious. This is exactly the *reverse* of what should happen! When pressure and stress levels get high, it is more important than ever that the briefings continue. In fact, in those instances it's actually preferable to shorten the gap between meetings and have them more frequently. When things are getting crazy and happening fast, that's all the more reason to keep everyone informed and motivated. There will always be a few people saying, "I just can't afford the thirty minutes out of my day to listen to this stuff," but in the end, everyone gains from the experience.

Keep the Team Updated with Email

In between your formal departmental meetings, use email for what it's best at: general announcements. Give your team a periodic update on cool happenings in your department and interesting activities around the company. If you're lucky enough to have a boss who does this broadly enough to include all your own employees, it can partially offset the need for you to send your emails. Plus, your team will appreciate the skip-level information. Consider this a recommendation for your own boss's suggestion box!

Moving On

All the tips in this chapter will improve your interactions with the bigger group, whether you're running a meeting, presenting to a larger group, or keeping your whole department up to speed. Now that we have these basics down, let's return to the area of one-on-one communications. One of a manager's most difficult jobs, and certainly one of the most important, is …

Chapter 4: Managing Performance

No matter how much management experience you have, handling personnel performance issues can be one of the scariest topics on the table. How can you be supportive and constructive without being weak and ineffective? How do you navigate a minefield of pitfalls to avoid being Mr. Dingus? You can come down too hard, you can fail to get your message across, you can apply inaccurate prejudices, you can inappropriately embarrass … and on and on and on. But when you find the right technique, you can both avoid the pitfalls and accomplish what you really want—getting your employees to improve themselves.

Just as with our discussion of presentations, I am not going to reinvent the wheel here. There are oodles of books that get deep into the guts of personnel performance management. Enjoy them! The purpose here is to discuss a few key pointers to pluck much of the lowest-hanging fruit, along with some tips that you probably won't read anywhere else.

Formal Performance Reviews

Let's start with the big one. Most companies have some sort of system for periodic, formalized performance reviews. It's understandable that a big organization would want an official report to file away. But if you've been doing your job well, the review itself should be pretty much a non-event. If you've been working and communicating with your team the way you should be, the formal review should be exactly what it says it is—a review. That means it should involve little more than going over and restating that which has already been said.

Proper Preparation

The formal review process generally begins a few days ahead of your formal meeting with the employee, when you get all the paperwork filled out.

Keep Score Throughout the Year

Review preparation will be a heck of a lot easier if you make a habit of keeping some sort of regular record for everyone on your team, jotting down any major positive or negative events or impressions for each worker as they happen. If you have even a few casual notes to which you can refer, you won't have to brainstorm everything at once—and most likely forget a bunch of key information in the process.

Hopefully, you also have some goal-planning procedures in place. If you have a list of solid, formal goals for each employee, performance-review preparation can almost take care of itself. (Check the "GOOOOAAAALLLL!!!!" chapter later in this book for a lot more information.)

Score Honestly at Review Time

On the review paperwork itself, you will almost certainly be required to score your employee according to some company-wide system. Those ongoing notes and goals I mentioned before will make it a lot easier to map your general experiences with the worker into Human Resources' entertaining mix of job ability and personal traits, like "decision-making skills," "initiative," "judgment," and "nice dresser." (I guess that last one falls under "decision-making skills" or serious lack thereof.)

Filling out the scorecard is easy when you're giving someone top marks across the board. But the idea of delivering the bad news can be somewhat daunting when you're dealing with anything less than a maximum score. Even a 4-out-of-5 score won't go over so well when someone is expecting the full "5" rating, and telling someone that he is only a "1" or a "2" can be very difficult. But you must resist the temptation to fudge your marks. In the long run, you'll only be hurting yourself and your team if overly generous scoring prevents everyone from reaching their full potential.

Of course, if you've done a good job of providing timely feedback throughout the year, everyone's review scores should be pretty close to what they expect. But even in the best cases, your formal delivery holds significant extra weight to your employees. The performance review probably maps directly into the annual merit-increase process, and these days, employees know that they need to score well if they have any hope of getting a raise. This is not a bad thing. Increases or bonuses that aren't tied to concrete results become ineffectual. But it places the extra burden on you to support your decisions.

No Surprises!

I already mentioned this at the beginning of the section, but I'll say it again: there shouldn't be anything to discuss in the formalized review meeting that you haven't already covered throughout the performance period. If you have something nice to say, but you haven't applauded the person for it in the entire year leading up to your sit-down, you need to reassess your positive reinforcement strategy, Mr. Dingus. On the other hand, if there are problems you need to discuss, and this will be the first the worker has heard of it, you have seriously violated the rule of timely correction. He'll have every right to wonder why you waited up to a year to finally let him know that anything was going wrong.

By the way, reviews can be a two-way street here. When you ask your worker for feedback on your own performance—you do that, right?—there shouldn't be any surprises for you, either. If he takes the opportunity to mention something he finds troublesome, and you have no idea what he's talking about, you probably didn't do enough to coax it out of him earlier.

Consistency Is Key

Getting through all this requires a heaping helping of honesty. But as I've said, performance reviews are not the time to fudge things for the better. If throughout the year you've been delivering the message that someone needs to take more initiative in his job, and that improvement hasn't happened yet, why wouldn't you transmit that exact same message now? Suck it up and assign the rating that indicates he needs to improve. If you don't, the message contradicts everything you've been attempting to communicate up until then. Plus, the worker will discover that any problems you have with him during the next year will be ignored when it really counts. That's not an incentive for improvement, and it can even lead him to question other aspects of your honesty down the road.

The bottom line is this: just as in every other communication, the review process is a time to be honest with your employee. It isn't always fun, but it's part of what you signed up for when you took the job. Neither overly negative nor overly positive ratings will allow you to accurately fine-tune your workers' capabilities and mentor them to be even better employees. Inaccurate ratings don't generate respect. And they make it harder to reach the ultimate goal: building a highly performing staff that trusts you to watch out for them.

Delivering Bad News

It's no challenge at all to deliver a review to your top worker. Anyone can pat him on the back and give him the best ratings with their eyes closed. Of course, you shouldn't shortchange him, and there will almost always be some suggestions you can make along with the affirmations. But the all-positive meeting should, in general, require much less time than the negative review—or any review where you deliver a rating that's lower than the recipient wants (or expects) to get.

I am always more "on my game" when it's time to speak with someone who is not one of my top workers. In my early management years, I was quite nervous going into those reviews. But eventually I realized that I was delivering an honest message that shouldn't be coming as a huge surprise. It was up to me to handle the event as something positive, even when I was bringing not-so-positive news. Now I look at these meetings as opportunities instead of something to dread. This is a chance to reiterate the points that the worker needs to comprehend and improve upon in order to progress overall. In fact, I'd actually prefer to have every one of my people dissatisfied with some aspect of his performance—even if it's "good enough" already. I want him to want to work on it with me to improve even further. That's the way you continually grow a team, no matter how good they are already.

When it's time to actually deliver the message, do it clearly, concisely, and with as many actual examples as needed. As with all one-to-one communication, try to make your meeting as much of a two-way dialogue as possible. Don't blame, but reflect upon the problems over the past year. Work with the employee to help him understand, again, how to improve his problematic traits. If the worker has any interest at all in improving his work, this is a great time to start turning it around.

Keep the Focus on the Individual

Sometimes when I'm delivering a less-than-stellar review, I'll get a comment like "Well, I think I do that better than Sam does." Any comment that implies comparison with another employee always gets exactly the same response from me: "We're talking about you, not Sam."

This is a simple, nonnegotiable requirement of any review—or any other communication you have with your workers. When I interview people for management positions, I always role-play them through some sort of performance review. As the "reviewee," I make a comment that compares myself to someone else. If the potential manager replies with any answer other than one like I gave above, it's an immediate disqualification. Never, ever, *ever* discuss relative treatment with respect to review ratings, salary, bonuses, or anything else. It's worthless, and it's unprofessional. And it can even get you into trouble on privacy issues.

Turn That Frown Upside Down

The intent of a negative review is not to make the recipient feel downtrodden and ready to jump from the roof the moment the meeting is over. Your goal is to get him to understand how he can make himself better over the next year—and for next year's review. On occasion, I've had someone say, in nearly these exact words, "Man, I know I suck at that. But I really do want to do better." I'm thrilled to hear that, and an open mind like that will get a big chunk of my attention in the future. On the other hand, comments like "I think I'm much better at this than you say" show a basic disconnect with the situation. You need to overcome that with concrete examples and—even more importantly—immediate feedback when it happens again to shore up your point.

But you don't want to deliver that message by simply saying, "You're wrong, and I can prove it." Instead, use something like

> "Hey, I hear you saying that you're not satisfied being average for this. You want the very top rating. That's great! I want to see you get there, too. Let me give you some additional pointers, and we'll work closely all through this next year. I'm confident that, if you take this seriously, we can get you there by a year from now. How does that sound?"

Remember that your team's overall ability is not a zero-sum game. You can have all your employees doing well. You *want* to have them all do well. Make sure the unhappy worker knows that. Help him understand that you're not bringing him down. You're giving him the "cheat codes" he needs to gain superpower status.

That Wasn't So Bad

If you've done your job right, the person you just reviewed will leave the meeting feeling uplifted, even if he needs to improve in many different areas. That's because, if you presented the review properly, your worker will understand how he needs to change and realize that you truly want to help him succeed. And he will know that doing so will lead to a markedly different outcome next year.

You will experience a big boost, too. It feels wonderful to genuinely help someone improve. And when you turn what could be a hairy, nerve-wracking brawl into a productive, friendly discussion, that will ultimately help you form a better team—one whose constituents don't see you as Mr. Dingus, but as someone who assesses them honestly and who cares about their future. You'll sleep like a baby that night.

Performance Managing with Fresh Eyes

Whenever I start a new position, one of my highest priorities is to speak with my direct reports and learn everything about them, their jobs, and (in the case of managers) their people. I also meet with my boss and my peers to learn how they see each of my people: who's strong, who's weak, who has untapped potential, and so on. And in many cases, my new boss tells me that I need to seriously improve the performance of one or more of my new team members. I might even be given the strong feeling that one of my new people may need to be managed right out the door sooner rather than later.

Assessing the Situation

When you take a new position, you certainly have plenty to learn. Make sure that one of your early priorities is to specifically request feedback on your people's performance. And then, after you have collected this data, you have a very important step to take: forget about it.

Okay, I don't really mean that the information should be 100 percent gone forever. Use the information you gather to help you get started in the right direction. But the word of other people, no matter how unanimous, should never be the sole input you gather about who might need to go. The primary determination should always come from data that you collect personally.

Nor should the decision be made too quickly. It is important to take your time with any decision that can have a major effect on someone, especially something that could be a career-ender. You'll probably need a couple of months to really see the worker

Shutting Up

in action and experience his ups and downs sufficiently to build up an opinion.

Of course, while you're gathering your data, your boss (or others) may ask, "What the heck is taking you so long?"

My reply is fairly simple:

> "Hey, if you really wanted to get rid of this person, why didn't you do it before I got here? Now I get to look the situation over. You may end up being right, but maybe there's a way to recover the situation. That would be a win-win for everyone."

Once you've had sufficient time, if your personal assessment matches what you've heard, then you can feel confident moving forward with some sort of performance-management action.

Seeing It Differently

But what if you don't see what everyone else has been describing to you? Your team might have described Jack as Satan himself—never following through, never being on time, never producing quality work, a terrible attitude, whatever. But you might see the complete opposite, or at least something much closer to neutral. How do you rectify the different viewpoints?

By earning your pay, that's how. Start looking into all of the variables. Was something wrong in Jack's personal life? Maybe Jack brought some personal problems to work some time ago, and he's gone back to being a decent employee. But he crossed swords with a bunch of people at the time, and they're having a difficult time forgetting it. Maybe Jack made a big error, eons ago. He's learned a lot since then, but the impression that he's incompetent is living on. Or maybe he just didn't get along with his previous boss. Now he's thrilled that you're there, and he's excited to show you what he's capable of.

I've actually witnessed each of these circumstances, along with many others. It can take some digging to figure out what's going on, and ultimately you may not be able to pin the "new Jack" on any single, obvious factor. That's when you need to ask yourself whether it really matters anyway. If you've got someone who seems to be a keeper—someone you think will help you and your team achieve your goals—it's up to you to stick up for him. Let his detractors know that you don't agree with them, and encourage them to give him another chance.

The point is, you are the new person in town. You have the job of assessing your team. You are the one with the fresh pair of eyes, not affected by anything that might have occurred in the past. It's your call. Don't be afraid to make it.

Back on Board

And there's a side benefit to handling this kind of situation with a "fresh eyes" attitude, especially if Jack's problem was something personal with his previous leader. When you have that first, long sit-down with Jack, he is going to assume that everyone has given you the full 411 on him. He's going to expect your relationship with him to pick right up where his previous boss left it. Instead, use the opportunity to get your new working relationship off on the right foot:

> "Jack, when I spoke with my boss and Human Resources, I heard that, over the last year or so, you've had a few performance problems. I can't discount those completely out of hand, but I would like you and me to start fresh. Let's do a quick review of some of the issues I've heard about. You can tell me your perspective, and we'll make

sure you understand how to improve on those items, if you haven't already. Then we'll put them out of our minds and look at the future."

Jack really isn't going to see that one coming. With luck, he's already been wishing he could get a fresh start, and maybe he'll take advantage of it. When someone who's built up a negative record learns he's already "out of the race" with you, he isn't going to try very hard to pull out the win. But if he's given an opening to start over instead, it may be just the opportunity for which he was hoping.

Sadly, that doesn't happen all the time. Some Jacks will try a bit, but then fall right back into their old ways. Others won't bother to try at all. With those people, you'll quickly see their performance live up (or down) to the negative expectations of your colleagues. But sometimes it turns out better than you ever hoped. And that's when you get a double positive: you gain a performing employee, and you gain his respect.

But He's Irreplaceable!

As a manager, you will almost certainly have a fairly constant flow of team members who require performance management. Hopefully, it won't be a big flow—if you're lucky, more like a trickle. But whether you have lots of people to manage or just a few, you may get hit with the doozy: when the targeted employee is someone who everyone knows is "one of the greatest minds on this planet" or "the only one who knows how the whole system works." But you can't excuse someone from performance correction just because he has a high IQ, he's been with the company since the dawn of time, or he's viewed as the only irreplaceable part of the whole. It still needs to be done.

If you're lucky, your troublesome guru will also possess the right attitude. He'll take your mentoring and correction efforts to heart, and you will measurably increase his overall positive effect on the company. But if you aren't so lucky, your worker will feel a little bit above the rest of the crowd, maybe even above your attempts to help him improve himself. Or he'll just have a bad attitude in general.

Making the Call

If the problems are fairly minor, it's possible that you can do your best but otherwise let it go. Your need to fully succeed is somewhat diminished if the worker is still contributing at a much higher level than most others.

But if the problems are major—if he's subverting processes, interfering with other people's work, or being downright disruptive and counterproductive—then you really have no choice but to improve the situation. And if you aren't successful at getting the worker to improve himself, you are going to face an incredibly tough decision. Do you let him go and say good-bye to maybe the only person you have who knows how everything works? Or do you hang onto him and deal with all of his detractions and distractions? Surely you can fix him eventually, right?

I have come across this situation a few times over the years, and I must admit that I took the latter course most of the time. I will also confess that it was *always* a mistake. I've had success with a quick turnaround more than once. But when I wasn't able to obtain improvement fairly quickly, and decided to stick it out anyway, I was never successful in turning it around further down the line either. Eventually, I was forced to make the tough call that I should have made much earlier.

The Aftermath

It's rarely easy to make that call, even when you know that you truly have no choice. But when I would finally pull the proverbial trigger, something interesting would happen. People would come out of the woodwork to thank me! Usually I learned that the depth of the troublemaker's actual disruptiveness had never become fully apparent to me, no matter how much digging I had done. But once he was actually off the team, the full picture would start to emerge: story after story about how he had slowed things down, behaved disruptively, and generally undermined team productivity. Wow.

I also found that no matter how much everyone seemed to think that the ex-worker was the only person who understood the whole system, that belief turned out to be completely bogus. Every time I have shed that kind of troublemaker from my team, many others have come forward with at least a reasonable ability to replace his skills. And these people were thrilled to have the opportunity to step up and show what they could do.

You will never win by waiting so long to make the tough decision. Any possible downside to losing the troublemaker is vastly outweighed by the benefits of eliminating all the disruption and distraction, and you'll be amazed by the ability of others to eagerly fill the gaps. And there's a side benefit: you'll show everyone that you are not afraid to make the difficult decision, and that you have confidence in the rest of the team to handle it. You're also making it clear that no one on the team is exempt from following appropriate processes and behaviors simply because he's been around awhile or he's managed to keep some information very close to his own chest.

The Dingus will put up with anything to avoid tough decisions. You won't.

By the way, if you do have a worker who seems irreplaceable, why not rectify that tribal knowledge problem before it actually becomes an issue? Even if your gurus are great workers and teammates, you never know what could happen down the road. It's rarely a good idea to allow that much expertise to remain so highly concentrated. Instead, work with your team to identify the "secret knowledge" and start cross-training your people as much as practical. It's just good insurance.

Handling Meltdowns

Everyone screws up at some point. Hey, we're human. We've already discussed some tips for dealing with workers who make mistakes or aren't as productive as they should be. But now we're talking about something more than one of your people making an honest technical mistake; we're talking about someone having a full-blown meltdown—a "personal foul," as it were, such as yelling at a customer or publicly insulting another member of the team. That behavior is inexcusable.

Now you must deliver correction to the guilty party. Under no circumstances can you let this behavior slide. If you let it go without getting involved, you are providing excellent positive reinforcement. So you must never assume that the incident was a fluke and that the behavior won't repeat itself. Not only will it repeat itself, it will become infectious. The way in which you react to correct the behavior will determine how effective the correction will be.

When (and Where) to Deliver Correction

The first and most important aspect of correction is to deliver it quickly but *privately*. Sadly, we have all witnessed poor managers jumping on people in a public setting. But no matter how big the mistake, this should never happen. If you just start blurting, it will serve only to inflame the situation and make a lot of other people uncomfortable. Instead, you must take the employee to your office, a conference room, or anywhere else where the two of you can have a completely private discussion.

If the problem is a relatively minor one, the discussion can probably wait for the conclusion of whatever activity is in progress. But for major missteps, such as blatant mistreatment of a customer or fellow employee, it may be appropriate to immediately but gently remove the offender: "Excuse me, Joe, could I speak with you outside for a moment?"

Use your best judgment to keep the situation from escalating. But either way, do not wait any longer than necessary to pull the offender aside. The entire event needs to be fully fresh in his mind—and your own. If you wait until tomorrow, or next week, the event will start to fade from memory. Perceptions will change, and you might even make room for him to deny that some part of the event happened at all. Act fast.

How to Deliver Correction

Once you've retired to a calm, private setting, it's time to at least somewhat salvage an unpleasant moment. Correction is necessary, but if you do it right, you can also grow your team member a bit.

Start by being nice. Screaming at him will get you nowhere. Instead, view this as a "learnable moment" for your employee. It's possible that he doesn't even realize he's acted inappropriately.

So treat this like the other one-on-one communications we've already discussed. Sit down face-to-face. Meet eye to eye. Keep the dialogue calm and factual, not emotional. Shut up, listen, and guide your worker where he needs to go instead of lecturing.

I usually open with something like "So, how do you think that went in there?"

He Gets It ...

Your employee's first response may tell you that he knows exactly what he did, he knows why it was inappropriate, and he has no intent to ever repeat his action:

> "Boss, I am so sorry about that comment I made. I knew it the moment I said it. He really pressed my buttons and got me riled up, but I absolutely should have controlled myself better. You have my word that it won't happen again, and I'm going to go apologize to him as soon as we get out of here."

That's great. Praise him for recognizing his mistake. But it's still important to provide a warning about the consequences of repeating his behavior. Summarize clearly, with the minimum words necessary to get your points across, and make sure he understands the potential consequences of another meltdown:

> "I'm glad you understand that speaking to customers that way is completely out of line and terrible for our business. I know you will control yourself much better in those situations from now on. But I have to be very clear, this can't happen again. That would possibly mean your having to leave the company. Okay?"

... Or He Doesn't Get It

Unfortunately, the correction most likely won't be quite so easy. Your worker probably knows he did something wrong, but maybe he doesn't realize the extent of the damage. Maybe he hasn't really considered all of the possible repercussions for his future relationship with that customer or coworker.

Now is the time to use your communication skills to draw him out and help him think through what's really happened. Do your best to avoid outright telling him what he did wrong. Just as with most other mentoring opportunities, he will absorb much more if he figures it out mostly on his own. Provide as much leading material as you need to drag him to the right place—open questions like "What do you think that customer might do now?" can help—but try to let him discover the answer for himself.

Then make sure to discuss the specifics. If your worker was rude or hostile to someone else, for example, make sure he understands how it probably made that person feel. *Be specific.* There is no room for generalities—that will lead to confusion later.

When you do reach an understanding, praise him just as you did the worker who understood immediately. And, again, be clear that the behavior cannot be repeated and that the consequences could be as serious as termination. If he misinterprets that, you've done about all you can do.

Finally, whether or not he immediately recognized his error, make sure to document it with Human Resources in case he does melt down again.

Be Sincere and Don't Sugarcoat It

In all communications, your level of sincerity has a big effect on how well your workers receive and log your overall message. Sincerity is particularly critical when you're correcting bad behavior. Your worker needs to realize that the situation is genuinely serious. If you think his inappropriate comments were actually somewhat funny, and he knows it, he isn't going to worry about it too much.

He might even repeat the behavior in the future to provide you additional entertainment. Keep it serious.

And just as with other one-on-one communications, always give him your full attention. If you're trying to tell an employee that his mistake was very serious, and you're checking your email while you say it, the message will be highly diluted.

Along the same lines, make sure that the gravity of your message isn't lost. That means you must avoid adding any extra fluff. For example, sometimes you may have the desire to soften the blow by applying what's been called the "Oreo Treatment": you tell him something positive about himself, then give your desired negative message, and then close with another positive. But when you're trying to deliver a message as serious as behavioral correction, this sugarcoating only dilutes your intended message.

> "Sam, you are an excellent employee and a great worker. You show up on time, work hard, and you're a great example to the others. You shouldn't yell at customers. You have a great future here, and I think you're going to be a key member of our company for a long time to come."

Did you even notice the correction there? Message lost. If you've been giving your workers sufficient positive feedback at regular intervals, he'll already know all that other stuff. You absolutely should be acknowledging your worker's positive points as frequently as possible, but not now. Keep on point.

Summing It Up

- Make correction in private.
- Deliver the correction as soon as possible following the event.

- Allow the employee to discover the error, if possible. But be sure his understanding is specific.
- Be completely sincere about your feelings and the consequences of repeated behavior.
- Don't sugarcoat the message.

Handling Errors

Okay, we've discussed an employee who had a meltdown and behaved inappropriately. But what about the worker who just made an honest error? As always, it's up to you to handle the situation appropriately.

First, use the same general style of communication that you used with the worker who melted down: private, immediate, sincere, and specific. But the first time someone makes a particular mistake, take it easy on him. Face it—he knows he blew it, and he's terrified. Your goal is not to make him feel any worse, but to make sure he learns from his mistake.

> "Hey, you're human. Things like this happen, and we'll get through it. I know you're going to help set things right as fast as you can. Let's talk about how you can learn from this."

Now begin the discussion. Your goal is to agree on changes that can help the worker prevent a recurrence of the error. Make sure he leaves your office with a positive outlook and a full commitment to never repeat his mistake. If this is the first time he's made that mistake, words like "if this happens again" really aren't appropriate. But if he has had this issue before, you have every right to make it clear that it truly can't happen again.

After you have spoken with the employee, consider whether you need to discuss it with the rest of your team. If other team members will have work to do to help clean up or adjust to what happened, you'll need to address that. When you do, remember that some people might already know what's happened, but others could be just learning about it. This requires some delicate handling.

When it's time for that team discussion, focus on displaying honesty, compassion, and leadership. Treat the situation as a team event, not an individual person's screwup.

> "Everyone, we had a failure of the XYZ system. Mistakes happen. We're human. But if we all work together, we can get everything going again quickly with minimal damage."

Treat the situation calmly and without blame. The team will most likely know or learn who's really responsible for whatever happened, but they will also know it wasn't malicious—and each worker will know that it could just as easily be his error next time. Your calm, reasonable attitude will make everyone feel better about what happened.

Using Performance-Improvement Planning

As a manager, your day-to-day goal will be to get the best from your team. Much of the time, you're dealing with immediate issues—brainstorming for a new project, keeping a current development on track, or responding to problems in the field. The everyday fracas certainly keeps us all pretty busy.

But from time to time, take a few days to step back, analyze your entire staff, and determine where your weakest points are located. Identifying your poorest performers isn't as exciting as picking out your all-stars, but it's just as important. The list may be blatantly apparent as soon as you ask yourself the question, or you can perform a rank-ordering exercise. Either way, figure out who makes up your bottom 10 percent or so.

Next, look at that group and ascertain whether they are truly underperforming. Maybe you've hired or trained such an awesome team that even the worst performer is far above average. Major kudos to you! This really does happen, especially in smaller companies and start-ups. It's also possible when you've actually been given the opportunity to put together the entire group to your own specifications.

In most cases, however, your bottom 10 percent will be below-average performers. If some of them are already on performance-improvement plans for whatever reason, good. If not, give the idea some serious consideration. Your goal is not to terminate anyone. Your goal—and the goal that will make HR the happiest—is to improve every member of your bottom 10 percent so they no longer *are* your bottom 10 percent. That would be a win-win-win for everyone.

Of course, when you enact a performance-improvement plan, it will produce a paper trail that will eventually justify termination should it become necessary. And if it does become obvious that someone cannot be saved, don't hesitate to do what needs to be done. But your goal should always be to improve the people you have, not start over with an unknown quantity. You have time and money sunk in the people you have. Even if they're underperforming, they know something about their jobs and how your team operates. And if you do have to replace someone, there are inevitable costs: a long hiring gap while you convince HR you need another person, dealing with recruiting and interviewing, and the eventual ramp-up and training time for the replacement. It is a much better return on your investment if you can keep the people you have.

Turning around your underperforming people makes a great success story, too. You have the tools. Now give it a try.

Moving On

Now that you've optimized your communication with your team, it's time to leverage that interaction into the best possible output you can get. Going beyond basic communications, there are many things you'll need to consider when ...

Chapter 5: Working with the Team

As a manager, your job—besides making your own boss look really, really, really good—is all about leveraging your own skills across your entire team and ultimately leading them to highly productive results. To make this happen, you need your people working together nicely, feeling empowered and trusted, staying motivated, participating in their own improvement, and basically all rowing happily together in the right direction.

Let's get things going from the beginning: getting the right team together.

Building the Team

When you take a management position, most of the time you'll be picking up an existing team—you were either promoted from within or hired to take over because the previous manager departed. In that case, use the techniques discussed throughout this book to assess strong and weak points, and then work with your people to improve the performance of the entire team. But when you get the chance to form your team from scratch, it's a whole different ball game. Now is your opportunity to "stack the deck" and get a huge jump on your future success. Run with it!

There are many considerations to keep in mind while you're putting your group together. Obviously, your chief goal will be to construct a well-rounded team with the skills and experience you'll need for your future projects. For that reason, it may seem logical to exclude candidates who lack direct, applicable past experience in the areas you need. But if you consider only that experience, you're at risk of overlooking some other key characteristics that could ultimately prove more valuable.

I Want Brains

What's more valuable than skills and experience? Let me start with an observation from my own management career. Over the years, I have seen people walk into positions in areas where they've had no previous experience whatsoever. (I've even hired some of them myself.) These people are working in industry verticals that are totally new to them, doing jobs they've never done before with no training or education. And they've been totally successful doing those jobs. How?

Raw freaking intelligence, that's how. I mean, what do we really learn in school anyway? We learn how to learn. And what do we learn at work? We learn how to do the jobs we have. Incredibly smart people know how to assimilate information, apply the same basic processes that exist in every job there is, work as part of a team, and produce results. If they're managers, they understand that they don't need to know how to actually do a specific worker's job from day to day. Rather, they need to lead and develop their people and give their teams the tools for success. Those managers are able to learn enough, over time, to have discussions at an appropriate level of detail to help the team be its most productive. Give me a smart, natural leader anytime.

In other words, for *whatever* you need in a team, find the smartest people you can. Choose the ones who have experience that's reasonably close to what you need them to do, and surround yourself with them until you're drowning in them (or you run out of budget). They will shock you with their ability to pick up the tasks at hand and generate great results for you.

The Smart Ones Who Disagree

Aaron Sorkin, the writer and creator of *The West Wing*, *A Few Good Men*, *The Social Network*, and numerous other successful movies and TV shows, wrote a great line for a management character on one of his earliest shows, *Sports Night*:

> "If you're dumb, surround yourself with smart people. If you're smart, surround yourself with smart people who disagree with you."

I remember that line to this day because I've always appreciated when my team members are willing to have a different opinion than my own. If you train your team members to act as yes-men who simply echo back what they think you want to hear, your team's experience and point of view will never be any broader than your own.

When you're building the team, keep in mind that folks who will openly disagree with you may tend to be on the boisterous side. That should come through during the interview process. With internal candidates, it can also be important to read between the lines, especially if his current boss or coworkers tell you that he's a "troublemaker," he's "heavily opinionated," or he "never wants to go along." Consider the possibility that, for your purposes, those traits could be good things! Ask the commenter for some specific examples. You might be willing to kill to get the person he describes. And if that opinionated troublemaker is the right fit for your needs, he'll probably find himself in a refreshing and complementary environment like he may not have experienced before.

But just finding the right people is not enough. Once you've added those great minds to your team, remember to positively reinforce their efforts to give you options, and play Devil's Advocate from time to time. We've already discussed how important it is to look for every opportunity to suck someone's brain dry *before* you let him know what your own opinion might be. This is even more crucial when you've got super-smart people, because their thoughts are simply that much more valuable.

One of my favorite bosses was fond of saying, "If you always agree with me, what do I need you for?" Fortunately, he didn't say that to me ... too much.

Motivation Is Critical

Keeping people motivated is one of your biggest responsibilities as a manager. You can have the most intelligent people in the world and give them every possible environmental advantage you can muster. But if they have no motivation to perform, you're sunk.

Motivating your team requires real work. You can't simply excite one person in one way and expect that to extend to everyone else; people aren't all enticed by the same thing. Instead, you have to learn what makes each person tick—both what he deems valuable and what doesn't matter to him. You can then play those factors off each other to determine a good approach for each individual. Some people want recognition. Some want plum assignments. Others want flexible work hours or similar benefits, and still others want a fun work environment. And some people just want money, in the form of either salary increases or bonuses.

I mentioned before that money, per se, is not usually a big factor for most people, unless they're simply not getting enough of it. But note that I said "usually." Though it hasn't happened often, I have absolutely worked with people whose entire world was driven by money. Those people would put up with almost anything at work, as long as there was a path available to an increased salary, a bigger year-end bonus, a special project bonus, or stock options. So while it's best not to assume that money is anyone's primary driver, don't dismiss the possibility out of hand when it starts to appear that it might be.

The Performance Formula

Question: Why is motivation such a big deal?

Answer: It is the largest single factor in a person's performance level.

Motivation? Really? Let me explain. I like to express the correlation of motivation and performance with a simple formula:

$$P = M^2AT$$

In this equation,

- P represents overall performance.
- M is the level of motivation.
- A is the level of inherent ability of the worker: his intelligence and job skills.
- T represents the tools available to the worker. (Think of tools as physical items, like computers, software, and bulldozers, as well as the general work environment, processes, training opportunities, and overall personnel support.)

Consider each of the variables on the right side of the equation to be a real number between 0 and 1, where bigger values are better. By extension, the maximum value of P, on the left side of the equation, is also 1—if M, A, and T are all 1, P is 1 too. Also note that the M factor is squared, which means it must be counted *twice* when multiplying all the items on the right side of the equation.

Your goal is to maximize each of the values on the right side of the equation. The larger you can get those numbers, the higher the total value when you multiply them together (don't forget to square the M factor!). As those numbers approach 1, you can boost your overall performance as well—as close to the "maximum performance" value as possible.

When you consider this formula a bit more closely, you'll notice that all three of the variables you control—M, A, and T—must be scored very high to result in an overall performance score that actually approaches 1. For example, if each of the three factors slips to 0.8—which still sounds pretty good—you've cut performance down to just over 0.4 (0.8 x 0.8 x 0.8 x 0.8 = 0.4096—remember that M is squared and therefore multiplied in twice). That's only 40 percent of what it could be! That's right: even if you have reasonable 0.8 scores across the board, it still results in an overall performance level that pretty much sucks.

I'll discuss this equation (and others) in much greater detail in the "Making Estimates" and "Maximizing Productivity" chapters later in the book. For now, I present it only to underscore how crucial motivation really is. Obviously, you'll always do your best to get highly "able" people, raising A as high as possible. And you'll acquire the best tools that you can, maximizing T. But motivation is the most heavily weighted factor.

So let's repeat the question: Why is motivation such a big deal? It's because pure motivation can help you overcome troubles with both A and T: basic lack of ability, poor tool sets, overly burdensome processes, lousy office lighting, the wrong kind of stapler, and just about everything else.

Motivating the Team

Motivation is critical in a much larger context than that of each individual worker, too. The overall level of motivation across your entire organization is itself a living, breathing, measureable entity.

So how do you pump up the motivation of the team as a whole? We've already discussed one way: good communication. Take every opportunity you can to communicate with your team through email announcements, hallway meetings, departmental get-togethers, and anything else that crosses your mind. When everyone is up to date on current events and future plans, and everyone knows they're working together toward those goals, it's a great morale booster.

But communication isn't everything. Look for ways to turn up the "fun factor" a little, too. Sure, work is primarily about getting stuff done. But why not have some fun while you're doing it? After-hours get-togethers for pizza or a trip to the ball game are a great start. Events during working hours—bowling, paintball, picnics—can feel like playing hooky! Even some minor office high jinks, like tossing a foam football around the break room, can make people a bit more eager to hop out of bed and head to the office each morning.

At one of my early start-ups, we used to haul the barbecue grill out onto the roof once a week and cook up lunch. One group would run to the store for hot dogs, burgers, buns, and chips. Another team would bring out plates and utensils from the break room and set up the area, and still others would do the actual grilling. (And some people just knew how to look really busy while the meal was being prepared!) Everyone would spend an hour together, hanging out in the sun, trying not to lose the Frisbee over the edge of the roof, and enjoying a common activity that didn't have a deadline. The environment was great for camaraderie and blowing off a little of the steam that built up from the fourteen-hours-per-day, six-days-per-week schedule we maintained.

Be creative. Even during the workday itself, small practical jokes, lighthearted ribbing, or a game of Hangman on the whiteboard can go a long way toward making each person feel like an integral part of an extended family. Of course, make sure everything stays within the acceptable boundaries of your Human Resources department. And keep an eye on the CEO's calendar—when he's scheduled to stop by, you may want to hide that foam football for the day.

Demotivating the Team

Unfortunately, motivation can be a lot easier to lose than it is to gain. More often than not, a team's motivation level will tend to degenerate toward the level of the weakest link. When one individual is highly demotivated for any reason, his attitude can act like poison on the rest of the team. In the mildest case, the rest of the team will pick up on his attitude and wonder, *What's wrong with him these days?* He might be a subtle, ongoing, low-level disruption, constantly wasting his coworkers' time and bothering people with trivial issues. In the worst case, he'll be walking around actively demotivating everyone else—loitering by the water cooler and asking passersby, "Doesn't it just suck to work here?"

In any case, you need to get your demotivator under control quickly. There are plenty of tips throughout this book. As is so often the case, solid communication is a good way to figure out what's going on and how to fix it. If his situation truly can't be improved, you may have to find a new employee. But act quickly and decisively. An organization's overall motivation level changes like the reverse image of gasoline prices: it comes down very, very quickly, but it takes forever to get it back up again.

Said another way, months or years of good grooming and solid management can be undone in days by a single demotivated worker. Get it under control quickly. The rest of your team will greatly appreciate you for either getting him back on board or removing the distraction from their lives.

Staying on Top of Things

The best possible way to ensure that you're always up to date with the latest details of your group's progress is to continuously circle from person to person and ask them for their current status. In fact, why not ask them if they got that memo about the TPS reports?

Are you kidding me? Despite the fact that you probably had a very strange look on your face after reading that first paragraph, I have known managers that actually operated just like that. Their people were constantly being interrupted from productive work to give Mr. Dingus yet another status update. But heaven forbid that the Big Boss might come along with a question and Mr. Dingus couldn't immediately reply with absolutely up-to-the-second status. "That would make me look really bad and out of touch!"

Don't Worry about "Insta-Status"

Well, not exactly. A good boss—and I would hope that includes you—understands that the team is constantly making progress and that status is constantly changing. So set your team up with your expectations about when you need to be specially alerted about something, and let them do their freaking jobs. Then you can catch up with your team in your regular meetings, and in between updates you can monitor whatever online tool they use to track progress. When your own boss asks about some project status, reply with the most recent version that you have. If you feel that more information is necessary, add a note that you'll send an update when you get new data. Then go back to your day. Chances are the information you already have is pretty close to current anyway.

If your boss insists that you're always absolutely 100 percent up-to-the-minute current with every project and issue that your entire team is working on, think about getting a new boss. Or, as politely as possible, ask, "Would you rather I constantly interrupt my people to check on every inch of progress that they make, or should I let them actually do their work and get the project done?" With luck, your boss will see that your approach leads to better overall productivity and let you go back to work. Maybe he'll even adopt the method with you and your peers.

Status Reports

Another good management practice is to require your team to submit daily written status reports. Oh, sorry, I was kidding again. Status reports are kind of like suggestion boxes: a sign of a sick organization and broken communications. Sometimes, of course, your own management chain will demand some sort of periodic status report, and it would probably be a good idea to comply. And such reports can have some value if they aren't required too frequently.

But for your own sake, and the sake of your team and the projects they're handling, consider whether you really need all those reports from your people before you can compose your own status report to pass up the chain. If you're working with your group the way you should be, you'll be capable of writing 90 percent of the report without any further input from your workers. Then you can use reports from your subordinates as a cross-check to what you've written. But if you're dependent on incoming reports to actually inform you of what's happening, or if anything in those reports surprises you, you'd better take a good look at your one-on-one and group communications again. You aren't nearly as in touch as you might think.

Management by Insertion

Many good managers like to stay up to date with their teams by exercising what has traditionally been referred to as MBWA: Management By Wandering Around. I am a definite fan of this practice. Personally, though, I think the word "wandering" makes it sound a bit too aimless. Instead, I refer to it as MBI: Management By Insertion. Think of MBI as an enhanced MBWA, with the goal of actually getting yourself involved in many short conversations over the course of the day.

Whenever you have the opportunity, go take a walk through your team's area. There doesn't have to be a reason. I make it a habit to perform this type of trolling at least twice a day, whether I have an "excuse" or not. So just stand up and go. You'll find a bunch of people with their butts plastered to their chairs, working right along. Don't interrupt them if you can avoid it. But there's a good chance that, as you circulate, you'll also happen to bump into a couple of hallway-style conversations.

Listen First!

When you encounter a discussion in progress, start tuning into it as you approach. If the conversation isn't work related, operate as you normally would to decide whether your participation is welcome. But if your people are discussing a work issue, wander up gently and start listening to what's going on. Note that I said *listening*. (The title of this book is *Shutting Up*, remember?) Your objective is to gather information first. Only then should you—maybe—add a bit of relevant knowledge or insight. So let the conversation proceed as long as you can without chiming in.

The first few times you insert yourself into a conversation like this, your team might not understand your intentions. Just tell them, "Hey, don't mind me, I'm just listening." It doesn't need to be a secret. Eventually, your people will almost stop acknowledging that you've arrived at one of these little parties. And that's exactly what you're looking for.

Much of the time, the result of your insertion will be completely "read only"—you will leave with information you might not have had before. That information includes, of course, the actual content of the conversation. But in addition to that, you will get a chance to see your team in action. You'll observe how different individuals contribute to the discussion and how they react to and interplay with each other. And your team will get their own read-only input: they'll see that you actually do come into the office for more than paperwork and meetings, and that you're genuinely interested in your workers and the tasks they're handling. Even if that's all that happens, your little office stroll has already been very much worth your time.

Adding to the Conversation

Of course, after you have observed the discussion for some time (silently!), you may have a fact or two that will legitimately add something to the discussion. Or you may detect a problem. Perhaps the team is beginning to address some issue that really doesn't need to be dealt with right now, or maybe you realize that they're operating from some basic assumption that is no longer true (or never was).

This is when you have the ability to earn your day's pay in just a few short minutes. Start by simply asking a few clarifying questions—exactly as we discussed for one-on-one communications right at the start of this book. Maybe the conversation already covered some issue before your arrival, or maybe your people are actually talking about a slightly different subject than you thought. Indeed, sometimes the clarifying questions will lead to clarifying answers that allay your concerns.

But sometimes your concerns will be confirmed by the answers provided. If your people are missing some facts or getting something wrong, understand that this is not due to any basic "dumbness" on the part of the team. It's far more likely to be a simple and fully reasonable lack of awareness. Complex projects have hundreds of dependencies, assumptions, and other factors that can change rapidly and are not within any one team's direct control. As a manager, you're privy to a broader range of information and you have access to additional communication channels. Now is your opportunity to share that extra information and help your team by inserting yourself, and your thoughts, into the process.

But wait! Won't your team think you're a Dingus for barging into all of these conversations completely uninvited? That depends on whether you execute the MBI properly or blunder along like, well, a Dingus. If you handle yourself gently and maintain a noninvasive presence until you absolutely need to go vocal, your team will grow accustomed to your observations. They will come to understand and appreciate that you want to see them in action, and they'll look forward to your visits as a chance to show their stuff. And in those cases when they really were about to go running off in the wrong direction, or when you reduce their burden by eliminating the need for a task they thought was necessary, they'll very much appreciate that you wandered by.

Meeting by Insertion

MBI doesn't have to be limited to conversations that you happen to stumble upon in the hallways. I routinely ask my team members what meetings they have scheduled over the next few days. Frequently I'll learn that they're planning a discussion of some topic that interests me—sometimes even a topic for which I feel my attendance is actually mandatory.

When that happens, talk to the meeting organizer personally

and work it out. A good meeting organizer will try to protect everyone's time and get a meeting accomplished with a minimal complement of people—just as we discussed earlier in this book. So talk it over with the organizer, and use your discretion wisely. You may find out that the subject really will be covered sufficiently without you. But, especially if the topic is something for which you will ultimately be responsible, you may need to be in on the discussion. If that's the case, get yourself added to the list.

Always feel free to train your team to know when you need to be involved, too. "Hey everyone, if anyone schedules a meeting on project X, please make sure I'm included." Then make sure you show up as scheduled!

Trusting the Team

Staying on top of things gets much easier when you have inherent trust in the team.

Many people feel that trust must be earned. But I feel that you shouldn't be hiring anyone that you don't feel you can trust from the start, and that in general you should trust someone until (and unless) he proves he's not worthy of it. When you show trust in someone, it empowers him to perform much more efficiently than if he was being micromanaged. Sure, nobody's perfect, and mistakes will happen. But when you allow a smart person to go "figure it out" on his own, knowing that you have faith in him, it will boost his morale significantly.

Please note that I'm not talking about assigning someone work that is far over his head. You would never trust a five-year-old to power up a table saw. But we discussed the possibility of failure before, back when we were talking about Tell, Sell, and Solo workers, and that maybe it isn't automatically so terrible. So if you've got a situation where failure isn't overly likely, and where failure wouldn't result in a mushroom cloud or missing finger, why not take a chance? When people experience failure, but survive and rebound from it, it makes them a lot more willing to take reasonable chances in the future.

Remember to work within the bounds of Tell, Sell, and Solo. Some people might not *want* too much trust. But when you can, try to push their limits a little. You will be growing that worker immensely.

When mistakes happen, remember that your workers are human. When someone fails, it isn't necessarily going to be of such a scope that you should immediately lose all trust in him. And even if it is, that doesn't mean you have to lose trust *forever*. Just be certain that when you decide to start trusting him again, you're doing it for the right reasons. You need to have something real to go on. In cases like this, trust needs to be re-earned.

Dealing with Team Changes

"The only constant is change." That old saying may be somewhat trite, but it's definitely true. If you are a member of a company or department that hasn't undergone some kind of reorganization in the last few years, consider yourself lucky. Well ... actually, maybe not. These days, business conditions are constantly changing. Fluctuations in the economy, variations in consumer desire, and a thousand other factors all in flux mean that most businesses need to morph to some degree at least every couple of years, just to keep their edge.

At a more micro level, within your team itself, change may be even more frequent. Even if nothing is happening on high to directly affect your charter, many conditions might cause you to switch things up much more frequently.

The process of building a new team structure is another one of those topics that has innumerable books to its credit already, and every industry and market calls for something a little different. I'm not even going to try to touch that here. But there's a lot more to reorganizing your team than just the structure. The planning and execution are both just as critical.

Working Up to It

When you're making changes to your organization, it is vital that you ease the affected population through the process. I have known managers who were fond of the Big Bang approach—and I'll admit, early in my career I was one of them. Big Bangers absolutely love rolling out the whole new group structure to everyone at once with no advanced warning to anyone. It always gets a lot of attention, but it also leaves behind a wide wake of shaken, dissatisfied, and de-motivated people. Not to mention the fact that, when the dust starts to settle, someone will invariably offer some postmortem suggestions that could really improve the new situation. With luck, the Big Bang Boss might take the hint and update the new structure. But the thought of looking dumb for missing something so obviously important is a pretty great demotivator.

Don't be a Big Bang Boss. Instead, concentrate on getting it right from the beginning. And that means getting feedback from affected parties *before* you make the modifications. Not everyone will have something to offer, but they'll all buy into the change later because they had the opportunity to look it over in advance. And they'll appreciate that you wanted to include them in the process.

What if someone does have a good suggestion, but it doesn't quite jibe with your main idea, or you've already progressed somewhat past that in your planning? It's your call at that point, but ask yourself if the value of the new idea would outweigh the bit of readjusting you'd need to do (and the additional communications you'd need to have with people you'd already run it by). If the idea is worth it, then you have the chance to improve your plan before you roll it out. Instead of getting yourself stuck doing some embarrassing catch-up later, you'll be doing exactly what you always do—getting maximum input on all major decisions.

Who to Tell

When you're running your new plan by the members of your team, the question isn't so much *who* to tell as *what to tell them*. It isn't necessary to share the entire plan with every person who will be affected by some part of it. Instead, restrict most people's knowledge to facets of the plan that are relevant to their positions and the feedback you want to get from them. When doing so, be sure to stress the confidentiality of your discussion.

> "Please do not discuss any aspects of this plan with anyone else. Many people have not yet been informed, and they need to have the discussion with me first. I am deadly serious about this. Do you understand?"

Sometimes those last couple of sentences are needed to really bring the point home. If someone decides not to heed your warning, and he somehow manages to avoid involuntary termination, that's exactly the kind of "earning your distrust" we discussed in the previous section. You'd be justified if you never trusted him again to keep a secret, and I don't need to tell you to leave him out of all reorganization discussions in the future.

Getting back to the "who" part of "who to tell," you should at the very least include

- Anyone who will have a new boss.
- All people who will have their working assignments modified to any reasonable degree.

- People whose work environment or location will be modified.

- Managers or other team leaders who will have new subordinates.

- Anyone who's getting promoted! (More on that shortly.)

- Anyone on your team who previously has shown excessive sensitivity to similar changes. (Some people don't handle change well.) You don't have to tell them much if the other "who" points don't apply; just make them feel comfortable that something's going to happen.

- Your own boss, who will almost always have suggestions, comments, or outright demands.

- Anyone on your company's management team that you trust to give you solid feedback. In particular, be sure to speak with someone in Human Resources if there could be anything controversial about your changes.

- Your significant other. A neutral third party who still knows something about your organization from the stories you bring home can be another great cross-check.

Handling a Promotion

When your new organization puts you in the happy position of promoting someone into a management spot on your direct staff, that newly minted manager is naturally going to feel somewhat secondary to your other managers at first. He's joining the management team—maybe the first one he's ever been a part of—and he is now a peer to people who were previously his superiors. You can fully expect him to feel a little anxiety at this prospect; he's going to be expected to have a mind of his own, and he'll have to be willing to debate, negotiate, and interact with his new peers at their own level. This can happen even when his new peers are totally supportive of him in the new role.

You can short-circuit much of your new manager's concern by presenting the new position to him as a team. Chances are everyone on your team interviewed him for the spot anyway. So why not let him know he's the winner as a team, too? Get your whole management group together, and then call their new peer into your office. He'll be a little stunned when he sees everyone in the room, but he'll quickly get over it when he hears you say, "We wanted to let you know that we have chosen you to join our group!"

Note the use of the words "we" and "our" in your congratulations. Those words are critical. They tell your new manager that it's the team offering him the job, not just you. It sounds simple enough, but it sets a tone for his participation that will ally him with the rest of the management team and get him feeling empowered much more quickly.

Making the Announcement

If you follow these tips, the full announcement of your new organization might feel like a formality more than anything else. By the time you actually go in front of the team to announce the changes, a good percentage of the people in the room will already know how it affects them. Nobody should ever hear a reorganization announcement and worry, *I wonder what this means to me.* The only people surprised in any way by your announcement should be those who aren't going to be substantially affected.

What about after the reorganization is completed? For the first few weeks, be sure to meet with the new teams much more frequently than you normally would. Sit in on team meetings and review how they are interacting with each other. Monitor the situation for any indications of trouble, and you'll be ready to make adjustments as they become obviously necessary.

Resolving Cross-Team Issues

Any group of people working on any project of significance will have occasional differences of opinion, complaints about each other, and sometimes outright near fistfights with each other. When you have smart people fighting hard for what they believe in, confrontations can be tough to avoid. People are, after all, mostly human, and eventually you're going to have to deal with human issues. Just like oil and vinegar, some people don't mix well, but they come together long enough to make a tasty salad dressing—or a successful product.

One of the toughest conflicts to deal with is when one team complains that another team is "not doing it right" or "making our lives tougher by doing it that way." That complaint isn't much different from when one of your team members is upset with another, and the fact that the target of the complaint is a completely different team shouldn't change your basic strategy. Use your management skills to work with the principal parties, guide them through a discussion, and try to get them to come up with something that works for both of them. Just as when you're trying to build a consensus within your own team, you want to avoid dictating a solution. The solution they come to cooperatively and without your (too obvious) assistance is more likely to work for both sides, and by reaching it themselves they'll more fully buy in.

The difference between resolving an issue between two people and two separate teams is this: when it's two teams, eventually you'll need to announce some sort of change to the affected teams as a whole. And when you do, the way you make the announcement

Shutting Up

will have a huge effect on whether everyone buys into it. If you simply broadcast the change in a departmental meeting or over email, it's going to look like *your* change—and not their change, negotiated and agreed to by both sides.

For example, you could announce the change like this.

> "We had a meeting with the XYZ department about all that extra paperwork they make us do. We know this has been causing problems with you being able to do your jobs. They have agreed to fix the process."

Now, your team will be quite pleased with you for getting this accomplished. No more paperwork! But they're certainly not going to have a warm and fuzzy feeling about the XYZ department. For all they know, team XYZ was dragged into this decision, kicking and screaming, and wholly against their will. Your team might still believe that team XYZ would rather see their own policies enforced, and that team XYZ couldn't care less whether your team is able to get their jobs done, finish the project, and make the company money.

Even though it's great to get the fix, it's almost as important to heal the wounds that might have developed during the heated discussions. These teams still have to work together, so you have to get them comfortable with each other.

The best way to accomplish this is to have the message come from the leader of whichever group is most obviously accommodating the change. Email is acceptable, especially if the teams are geographically separated, but an in-person announcement at a departmental meeting of your own troops is even better. If the announcement comes from the party that's perceived as giving in, people will be much more likely to believe that his group has fully bought into the change. That seriously reduces the chance of any lingering hard feelings. If the leader presents the announcement in a really positive way, he can make his team's new attitude crystal clear:

> "We heard you, and we realized that the policies we had in place were way too imposing on you. We thought it would work okay, but we see that it's not. We'll be changing this quickly, and we'll get you what you need."

Now, keep in mind that the presenter may *not* have actually bought into the change. Indeed, he might have been beaten into submission and the decision forced down his throat. In that case, it is even more important that he delivers this message personally and in a positive way. And what does he really have to gain by being grumpy about it? He'll come across as a cranky, powerless wimp who doesn't give a crap about whether the company succeeds or not. He just wanted everyone to follow his inflexible and obtuse policies.

Of course, there's another caveat. Remember that sometimes the leader of the team that's accommodating the change is going to be *you*. When that happens, insist that you be the one to announce it to the affected parties. Even if you were forced into the final decision at gunpoint, make the announcement with the best smiley face you can muster.

At some point, you'll have to explain the change to your own team, too. And they might not agree with it either. We'll talk about that in the "Getting Respect" chapter.

The Team Is Your Extended Family

In many ways, the people you work with are like members of your family. Even if you aren't a workaholic, sum up the amount of time you spend at work versus the time you spend at home (while awake) and it will become clear. And many of the ways you communicate at home can apply at the office as well.

For example, is there a place for tough love at the office? You bet your bippy. We're not talking about sending someone to the corner, although I've certainly been tempted at times. But when the situation calls for it, you'll need to give difficult-to-hear feedback or even a full dressing down, just as you'd do for your own children. It doesn't mean you don't care about the employee; it means the employee's behavior isn't working for him or for you.

Another familial parallel for the workplace is the old trick of "don't tell our parents." I've had a few workers who went a bit crazy during an interaction with someone else. During our postmortem talk (remember the section about delivering correction?) I asked, "Would you have done that if I was there?" Sometimes the answer was yes, in which case I used the correction techniques we've discussed to help him figure out where he went wrong and groom him for a better outcome next time. But most of the time, if the worker was honest with himself, he realized that my presence would have caused him to be a smidgen more careful and maybe measure twice before cutting once. Given that, my advice was this:

> "Always pretend I am in the room with you, on the phone with you, watching you type your email, or standing next to you when you are speaking with others. Handle yourself in a manner that you know would make me proud."

Pretending that Mom and Dad are watching in real time is a pretty good buffering mechanism for a lot of bad behavior, from pushing too hard for an untenable solution to dishonesty to outright disrespect. The worker knows it's going to get back to his "parents" eventually anyway. So teach your people to avoid it to begin with, and make you proud.

Moving On

At this point in our discussion, you're putting your great communication skills to work and guiding your people to do their jobs and work together to maximum performance. How we work is important! But ultimately, our jobs as managers usually boil down to ...

Chapter 6: Making Decisions

Throughout your management career, you will make countless decisions. Some are major, some not so much. But nearly all of them will have some bearing on how you can optimize your personal success—and, more importantly, the results from your team.

The strategy and politics behind decision making on any particular subject can be analyzed enough to fill shelves of books on the topic. Here, I will hit on a number of different areas and highlight a few unique concepts that I hope will provide you with some good bang for the buck.

We'll break the discussion of planning and decision making down into four major parts over this and the next three chapters. First, we'll cover decision making as a way to get yourself and your team focused on the proper activities. Then we'll move on to estimating: predicting the amount of time and money you'll need to get things done. Next, we'll discuss decisions you can make to maximize your team's productivity, and what that can really do for your bottom line. Finally, we'll talk about setting proper goals for your team.

Before You Decide

Before you even think about actually *making* a decision, there are a few considerations you should have on your radar. These fall into three main chunks: maintaining focus, reviewing the context of each individual decision you make, and being ready to act decisively.

My Favorite F-Word: Focus!

If there's one single word that's been the mantra of my career, it's *focus*: the ability to home in on what's really important while ignoring the static. Focus is a key component of success. And when circumstances or other people attempt to pull your focus away from what's really important, you must push back as much as required.

But how does focus tie into decision making? Simply, you need to ask yourself a question before you work on making the decision: Could the result of making an incorrect decision here cause the team to lose focus?

For example, imagine your team is responsible for a big, important product that generates all the profit that your company ever sees. What happens when you're asked to divert some of your team resources to a nearly insignificant side product? I've seen managers on huge projects loan some of their people over to a small and unimportant task, simply because someone asked for help and they wanted to look like team players. But by doing so, those managers risked some aspect of a big delivery that was critical to the company. If your major project ultimately fails because you were a good corporate citizen who loaned key resources to a less important task, no one's going to remember that you were a good team player. All they will remember is that you screwed up the big one.

I know it seems like a pretty hardball way to play the game, and I'm not suggesting you must automatically veto any request for help that you receive. But to ensure overall success for your project, your company, and yourself, you have to stay focused on the tasks that truly demand it. If your boss asks you to divert resources or otherwise take your focus away from the task at hand, you owe it to him, your team, and the company itself to make absolutely sure that he understands how the change will affect your project. Is this other task really worth the risk to your core project?

And don't let anyone artificially boost the perceived value of some task in an effort to divert focus there. Television news stations are famous for attempting to enhance the attraction and excitement of their stories by throwing more cameras, on-scene reporters, and helicopters at them. But doing so does not change the inherent nature of the story; it just blows it far out of the proportion it deserves. The same is true for office distractions. Just because someone thinks that a certain task deserves its own helicopter does not necessarily make it so. Keep the focus, and help the rest of your team to keep their focus too.

You will always have numerous tasks and projects competing for your time. But the old 80/20 rule nearly always applies: only a couple of your projects are going to account for the vast majority of your success or failure. Keep your attention on the 20 percent of your projects that generate the 80 percent return, and consider the rest to be bonus items. Work on those bonus items, or work on making them better, if you have the time. But don't take your eye off the ones that really count.

Beware the Chain of Errors

Any time you need to make a decision, especially one that follows a series of past decisions, it's important to stand back and examine where your successive choices are taking you. No decision is made in a vacuum. But sometimes we run into a version of that old "forest for the trees" problem. We're so focused on the nearest tree that we forget we're in the middle of a forest.

When I was learning to fly, my flight instructor repeatedly warned me that we must always be on the lookout for the beginning of a "chain of errors." What did that mean? When you make a decision that could have a bad result, the negative consequences of that single decision may seem minor. And rarely will one single decision cause your project to fail disastrously. But what if, before you make the next decision, you take into account all the decisions you've already made up to that point? When taken together, the full context of your next decision might be cause for you to reconsider.

Consider an example from the aviation world. A long transatlantic flight is nearing the halfway point of its journey. The "point of no return" is approaching rapidly—the point at which the fuel supply is no longer sufficient to return to the departure airport, and the flight is committed to continue to its destination. The pilot must decide whether to continue or turn back. He notes that the headwinds have been much stronger than forecast, and the fuel supply now appears just adequate to reach the destination. He could decide to continue the ocean crossing based on that one point: "We have enough fuel to make it." On its own, that isn't a terrible idea. But on the other hand, what if a few other things have already gone wrong on this flight? Maybe one of the navigation instruments isn't functioning properly. Maybe the weather is getting worse near the destination, and there's a possibility that the flight will need to divert to an alternate landing spot.

Did the pilot take an unnecessary risk when he continued the flight after those first issues popped up? Maybe not. But these things add up. Now, when he considers whether to continue in the face of the huge headwinds, it's time to say "Stop!" and go for a refueling.

Fortunately, luck sides with us more often than not. But remember: just because you got lucky doing something ridiculously dangerous in the past does not mean that your luck will continue. One of these days, the laws of probability are likely to catch up with you.

Similarly, I often ask myself, "How will this look in the incident report?" Before you make any individual risky decision, imagine that you are writing a postmortem of your actions the next day. When someone reviews your description of everything that happened, how will it look to him? Will he laugh and shake his head in amazement that you could have ever made *that* decision under *those* circumstances? How would you feel reading the same report if it was written by someone else? "What an idiot! I would never have made that error." Thinking over the incident report before it happens can trigger you to examine your situation more completely and make it easier to recognize when an entire chain of poor decisions is leading to your ruin.

So don't be that idiot! Before making a big decision, always step back and consider the broader context of the entire project. Take into account all the choices that you and your team have made up to that point. Then you can assure yourself that the next decision is the right one.

Act Now!

Sometimes I'm amazed how long people are willing to let things ride, even when there's massive evidence pointing to a need for change. But staying the course is a pretty human reaction. When you're having a personnel problem or a process problem, or there's something inherently wrong with a product, it can be a lot easier to take the path of least resistance instead of making the tough call to change something. But inertia is poison to a well-functioning team.

As the leader of your team, you must remain as vigilant as possible against the tendency to hold course even when there's an iceberg in your path. And this is another place where shutting up and listening can be far more valuable than immediately talking over anyone on your team who's brave enough to point out the problem. Even the occasional outsider, benefiting from having a fresh pair of eyes, might simply ask, "What's up with that?"

When you detect things going wrong, through any mechanism, do not delay in finding a better way. It can be terribly tempting to avoid the extra work and put it off until tomorrow, next week, next month … especially when you're already busy. But even small problems don't fix themselves. Like cracks, they just get bigger and bigger, until eventually you're dealing with a monstrous sinkhole that requires a dump truck full of concrete to fill it. In the long run, wouldn't you rather apply a little caulk as soon as you see the crack?

Be especially wary of the potential for cracks to begin developing any time you are intentionally making changes. It makes sense—change is usually stressful, and stress causes cracks. So even when the changes are "done," keep a close eye on how things are working. You're already focused, so don't take your eye off the ball until you've seen solid evidence that your improvements are, indeed, improving things.

A general rule of thumb: Whenever you find yourself wondering whether it's time to make a decision about something, it's probably already *past* the right time. So just do it. Now.

But If It Ain't Broke …

Before you decide to implement changes, however, make sure that you're doing it for the right reasons. Go over the evidence, and confirm that it supports the need to do something different. In the past, I have definitely been guilty of making changes (or being talked into them, which is still my fault) when the situation didn't really seem to require modification at all. When I looked back after collecting additional information, it still wasn't clear that the change had made any improvement to the situation. Lesson learned: "If it ain't broke, don't fix it." Clichés become clichés because they're true.

... Will This Really Fix It?

There's also a corollary to "If it ain't broke." "If it didn't work before, why would it work now?" That one can sometimes be rephrased as Einstein's famous definition of insanity: "Doing the same thing over and over while expecting different results." If you stopped using a certain process, or terminated some employee, there was presumably a reason for that decision. If you're now considering going back to that process or rehiring that person, be sure to ask yourself *why*. What's going to be different this time? Will the process be used in a different environment? Will there be better people executing it? Has the old employee changed or grown somehow? Whatever the case, be certain that you're not expecting things to be different simply because some time has passed.

Decision Types

Okay, you've checked your focus, reviewed the context of the upcoming decision, and determined that there is a need to act. You're ready to actually make the decision. But the process of making the decision itself can be different depending on the type of question. Although there are a wide variety of decision flavors that you'll encounter, they tend to fit into a few fairly simple groups. Let's take a look at some special considerations for each of those.

The No-Brainers

If I had a nickel for every time someone told me that a decision was a no-brainer, I'd ... well, I'd have a lot of nickels. But as a manager with responsibility for your entire team, you need to take every decision completely seriously. Don't take shortcuts and make yourself the no-brainer by dismissing any possible choices completely out of hand.

Sometimes everyone knows that such-and-such course of action is entirely obvious. You look feeble spending time debating that issue with yourself. Really, it's that obvious. It's an absolute no-brainer. Why are you bothering spending any time on that?

Error! Henry Louis Mencken once said, "For every problem, there is a solution which is simple, clean, and wrong." This is when you need to be sure that you *have* adequately considered all your options. It doesn't have to take forever. Even a few minutes can be enough. And you might have already done most of the thinking you need to when you thought about the context and the chain of errors. But sometimes, even a few minutes' extra consideration can reveal an alternative path that, even if it doesn't prevail in the end, adds something to your pool of knowledge and experience. And that new addition might serve you well, allowing you to make better decisions in the future. You'll also find that when you allow new doors to open like this, and encourage your team members to think through some of the possibilities with you, they will gain from the experience as well.

The fact is, even no-brainer decisions usually require a brain. But note that I said *usually*. Once you've given the obvious solution a sufficient chance to disprove itself, it's time to move on.

The Shades of Gray

As a decision-making manager, you will encounter many problems that give you a choice between two seemingly distinct options: "We do X or we do Y." But even if X and Y are possibilities, neither is usually the best answer. There's almost always something in between X and Y that would result in a better final outcome. Welcome to the shade of gray.

Shutting Up

Gray is a beautiful color. But gray decisions can be tough because, face it, it's usually much easier to settle on X or Y. Then you don't have to spend extra brain cycles trying to figure out if there might be something a little bit gray that's more attractive—and if so, which precise gray is the *best* gray? But this is a pain you must accept. In my experience, black-or-white answers are usually insufficient to solve a problem. Worse, they may be outright wrong. Find the shade of gray that works better.

There Are No Small Decisions ...

Over the lifetime of a particular project, its success will be determined by how you and your team handle a huge number of decision-making opportunities. You'll make hundreds, even thousands of decisions as you plow the road to eventual victory or catastrophe. A few of these decision points will be biggies—major choices with huge consequences, for better or worse. But the vast majority of the decisions you face will be the small issues that you need to handle almost daily throughout the project life cycle.

Which of these decisions has a more urgent need for your thoughtful attention: the bigger ones or the smaller ones? The answer might not be what you expect. That's because the really big decisions are going to get *everyone's* attention. Your team will see the issue's significance so clearly that the pot will boil over with attention. As a result, it's actually more likely that the project will fail from a death by a thousand cuts, because no one is interested in those small decisions. And none of those little wounds will attract the same level of interest as the big issues ... until their cumulative toll has the whole project in deep trouble. So make sure that those hundreds or thousands of small issues get some attention directly from you.

As an aside, this is an area where the MBI we talked about earlier can really come in handy. When you're locked away in your office, you won't stumble onto the minor issues when they pop up in spontaneous hallway conversations and various random meetings. But when you get out into the middle of the action, it makes it possible for you to catch those smaller issues as they go by. And that will give you that much more opportunity to help your team make quick course corrections.

... But There Are Complicated Ones

Some of the biggest, most complicated decisions we need to make are when it's time to guess how much time and money it's going to take to complete a project. We'll dive in there in the next chapter, where we discuss ...

Chapter 7: Making Estimates

The ability to make accurate predictions is a highly critical aspect of your job as a leader. And some of the hardest predictions to make are project estimations. When new work is coming your way, the management chain is going to want to know how long it will take. If you're working in an industry that can take advantage of an AGILE process, you can avoid many of the problems involved with estimating very large projects. But if you're using a more standard process, your ability to intelligently provide an overall estimate that comes close to reality will do much to solidify or liquefy your management career.

If only it were so easy! When you're estimating a project, there are always countless variables in play—both the requirements you have to produce and the assets you have to make it happen. Then add enormous pressure from above to deliver absolute maximum performance with a minimum of expense and time. When you're in the midst of it, the project-estimation experience will frequently leave you wondering what you ever thought was so enticing about a management job in the first place.

As with so many topics we've been covering, there are oodles of texts available that cover a multitude of processes for generating accurate estimates. However, over the years, I've found that keeping only a few key principles in mind can help make the job much easier. And I'll share a few tips to help you deal with the constant pressure to do more with less—and to discover how maybe you can.

We'll start by covering the cardinal rule of guesstimating.

Overestimate and Overdeliver

If you do only one thing right when you're estimating a project, this is the one. Always, always, *always* leave plenty of room for your team to adequately get the work done. If that sounds like a no-brainer to you, consider that it can sometimes be incredibly tempting to deliver estimates that make it look like your team can perform at superhuman levels. Maybe they even can, from time to time. But when you give those Superman estimates too often, it will lead either to failure (if you're lucky) or to utter mutiny as your team grows to resent the never-ending pressure you're placing on them. A good team will step up to the plate for you in an emergency situation, or when the company might have a major opportunity. But if you constantly make them work eighty-hour workweeks so you can come off as some kind of hero, you're heading into Dingus territory fast.

When you're sure you've left sufficient time in your estimate to allow your team to accomplish its goal without absolutely killing themselves, you most likely still need to provide a bigger safety margin. Even the best-run projects have a tendency to take double the time you expect, and that's assuming that your estimate landed somewhere in the right ballpark to begin with. If you were even a little bit off, the problem will get worse quickly.

Making the Estimate

Here's a general overview of the estimating process: start with a

Shutting Up

good estimate, pad it for safety, discover you were estimating the wrong thing, adjust your estimate and padding, and finally take flak from above for having such a large estimate. Sound about right?

Here's the key fork in the road: When the flak comes, will you succumb to pressure and reduce your estimates, even if you know you shouldn't? Or will you support your estimate with solid information and stick to what you know to be true?

Let's walk through each part of this.

Gather Self-Estimates

The best way to estimate the time it will take your team to accomplish a task is not to estimate it at all—not by yourself. Instead, let your team give you their estimates. Start with the frontline people who will actually need to do the work, and ask them for *their* best estimates. They're the ones with the most intimate knowledge of what they're being asked to do anyway. It is also usually true that workers will give themselves tougher goals to achieve than you would assign for them. Whether they desire to overdeliver, their egos want to prove something, or they just know how to do something better than you do (hard to believe, I know), whatever estimate they come up with is the one with which they feel comfortable.

At this point, each worker owns his estimate. As long as you don't go messing with the assignment, he should be absolutely committed to coming through for you—no excuses. If that means he needs to work a little extra time, okay. Keep your eye on his progress, and make sure to refresh his memory if you need to. There is absolutely no excuse for someone who makes his own estimate of 10 days to take 10.5 days to deliver. If at the end of that tenth day, you see that worker heading for his car at 5 PM, congratulate him on having the job done on time. If he says, "Actually, I just have a few more hours to do and should be all done by lunch tomorrow," you have every right to turn him around and send him back to his desk. He couldn't find an extra few minutes each day to get it done? Not acceptable.

Major project slippage doesn't happen all at once. It's the result of many little slips all piling up on each other. Mind the little things.

Pad the Estimate ...

Once you have all your estimates, roll them together until you have a total, and then apply a safety factor. But don't go sandbagging your estimates—you know, intentionally padding everything far beyond anything reasonable. Remember Scotty from the old *Star Trek* TV series? When he appeared on *Star Trek: The Next Generation*, he admitted that he always grossly inflated his estimates so that he could always be the hero for Captain Kirk. But this isn't *Star Trek*, and you are unlikely to have as much success with this technique as Scotty did. Sandbagging has a way of becoming very visible and very unpopular, and people who rely on it usually have a fairly short life span in the real business world.

But how *do* you know how much extra to add? Experience! Estimation takes practice, and it's something you can grow more comfortable with as your career builds. But that's not the only experience I mean. A good estimate will also have a component that's specific to each particular team that you lead. Every different group, every different company, every different product, every different set of processes—they all create their own environment that requires a different amount of "fluff" in your estimates. With experience, you'll learn how accurately each of your team members can estimate his own work. (That ability, in itself, is a highly valuable skill to watch for.) Over time, you'll learn who needs bigger safety factors and who is pretty good at nailing it time after time. And keep tabs on those accurate estimators. You might want to start grooming them for additional responsibilities in the leadership realm.

Don't let anyone tell you that you're cheating by building in a safety factor. You're being smart. There's nothing wrong with adding padding that represents what you have truly needed in the past. Any good manager understands the need to account for estimation errors, compensate for requirements that you expect to change along the way, or prepare for the occasional disaster. And it's easier to build it in early on than it is to try to readjust everything later.

That's not cheating. That's using your experience to lead your team to a successful conclusion.

... But Don't Go Crazy

Ultimately, your goal should be to overdeliver on whatever your leadership thinks you've actually signed up for. Coming in a little early on that deadline, or adding a few more nuggets of gold to the product than they expected? Terrific! But note that we are *not* talking about overdelivering by some massive amount—only by a little. Yes, sometimes the stars will align and everything will go close to perfectly, leaving much of your padding time untouched. That's a nice treat. But if you consistently deliver in half the time you predict, people will start to think that you're trying to be Scotty and look like the hero. Even if that isn't your intent, take it as a sign that maybe you're padding things up a bit too much. Realize that something is different in this environment than in the one you were using as a model, and tweak your algorithm a bit.

"Isn't it great, though, if I can constantly deliver much sooner than I've predicted?" No! Scotty-like heroics notwithstanding, there are many other people and teams who are using your estimates to build their own plans. They're weaving together tasks from a number of different projects, and if you keep coming in that early, you're going to make them miserable. Their workload will spike with peaks and valleys just when they thought they had everything smoothed out. They will not be your friends.

"Yeah, but at least the sales folks will love me!" Nope. Your sales team probably won't mind a delivery that's a little bit early. But if you are *really* early, they won't yet have prepped potential customers for the arrival of your bouncing-baby product. You'll throw it over the wall to them, and their reply will be "I have nobody ready to buy this right now." They won't be finished with the marketing brochures, advertising, and other sales support they'll need to have available, and your support department won't be staffed up yet to deal with the influx of customers.

In short, crazily inflating your estimates doesn't help anyone—not even yourself. Use a reasonable safety factor, and then target your work to overdeliver by just a bit.

What Were We Doing Again?

Okay, you've taken the requirements. You've analyzed your group's capabilities. You've—uh, wait a minute. Let's go back to that "requirements" thing. When you made your estimates, what requirements, exactly, were you basing them on? Did you actually have real requirements to work from? Or did you just get something like "We need a product to do online banking" or "We need a new parking structure on that corner" or the like? Gee, those are pretty big tasks, and there are about a million different features and capabilities that you may or may not want to include in one of those projects.

If you're working in something like the construction industry, the actual requirements are much more likely to be at least fairly well nailed down at estimation time. But in many other industries, this might not be the case. If the requirements for your project can't be well enumerated to you before you make your estimate—or at least before you deliver it—make sure that you at least document the assumptions that you made as part of the estimating process. Even the process of recording those assumptions can help to clear up some ambiguities a little bit earlier.

Of course, if you're working in something like the software industry using an AGILE-like process, the lack of clear up-front requirements is the norm. But if that's the case, you probably aren't being asked for long-term estimates anyway. If you do need requirements and don't really have them, cover your butt by being clear about exactly what features or functionalities are included in your estimate.

Expect Pushback

So you've considered the requirements, mapped your group's capabilities, gotten bottom-up work estimates from the folks who know best, and applied a reasonable set of safety factors. Good work! You have arrived at an overall estimate with which you are comfortable. You honestly feel that your group has a pretty good chance of getting the work accomplished, in a quality manner, within your time estimate.

Buzz! Sorry, thanks for playing. Your estimate, in almost all circumstances, will not be good enough for your top leadership. They need it sooner. Whatever the reason—to grab an important prospective customer, to beat a competitor to the punch, to come through on some promise you don't know about, or just because they don't think you put enough thought into the estimating process—they need it sooner. Be assured that this will be the case even if you've gone completely out of your way to squeeze every bit of slack out of your estimate, and even if you've used absolutely minimal safety factors. Your estimate will always be too big. Get used to it.

Sometimes, when you go back for round two of the estimate, you might actually find a few items that you can tighten up. And you might be able to rethink some of your safety factors. But at some point, when you feel that you've done your honest best, you're going to have to stand behind your estimate—and in all likelihood it will still be too big. Highly entrepreneurial leaders are especially likely to demand the near impossible, and they're going to do everything they can to convince you that what they are asking for has to be done. That's a good time to remember that just because you or your boss want it doesn't necessarily make it possible. It may not be possible even if you simply have no alternative. The working world would be a much easier place if it were so. But it's not.

All of our needs have to be tempered by reality. But you aren't going to get anywhere if you respond to requests for "more stuff in less time" with subjective comments about how you've already done your best. Sooner or later, you'll find yourself pressured into signing up for more than you believe to be reasonably possible. And then, when the project ultimately fails to meet the deadline, nobody will care that your original estimate actually represented reality fairly well. You signed up for the schedule, and you failed.

Good managers don't send their people off on projects that everyone knows are beyond their limits. At that point, even the team's best efforts probably won't be sufficient. That kind of attitude morphs into low motivation, and that pretty much dooms the project before it's kicked off. And it makes you a Dingus for agreeing to it.

So what can we do? We have to find a way to bring science and objectivity into the discussion to strengthen your ability to resist the pressure from above.

Supporting Your Estimate: Balancing the Variables

We've all heard the adage about project estimates being analogous to three-legged stools, where the legs represent content, budget, and quality. Sometimes, people will refer to this belief with the quip "Content, budget, quality: pick two." They mean that you can lock in any two of the factors and then calculate the third. But I have found this to be an overly simplistic view of the many variables that affect project estimation.

Over the years, I have developed a formula that calmly, quietly, and scientifically brings order to the discussion of how to get the most work done in the least amount of time. More importantly, you can use it as a tool to consider possible trade-offs that you can make to get your project done in the time frame that your management demands.

Bear with me, as we're going to do some math. Don't cheat by skipping it! It isn't hard math, and the result will be some amazingly simple and powerful relationships that may change your entire perspective on project planning and personnel management. Buckle in—this won't hurt.

The Formula

We will develop several different versions of this formula as we dive deeper into our discussion, but let's begin with this edition:

$$\frac{CQ}{BS} = k$$

In this formula, the following values are represented:

- The amount of content, features, or some other measure that indicates the raw size of the job. "How big is this sucker?"
- The quality level of each part of the content. "How well is each thing going to work?"
- The available budget, expressed as a run-rate value, such as "dollars per month" or "people assigned."
- The schedule, expressed as some period of time. "We have how many months to get this done?"
- For now, think of k as some constant value for your particular organization.

Expressed in words, this formula states that for the constant k, the items above the line—content and quality—must always remain in proportion to the items below the line—budget and schedule. If you want to increase any of the four values, you must either decrease the value of the neighboring variable or increase one of the variables on the other side of the fraction separator. Period.

Doing Some Real Balancing

For example, say you want to get more content into the product—an increase in C. You can do that, but only at the expense of reducing quality (Q), adding more people (B), or extending the schedule (S).

Think about that more closely for a moment. The last time you were asked to add additional content to a product already under development, did you ask, "What can I pull out in exchange?" (thereby keeping the same total C) or "Can I have more people on the project?" (increasing B)? Maybe you responded, "I'll need more time," thereby increasing S.

But have you ever asked, "Is it acceptable for us to lower the level of quality in the final product?" That may sound silly at first, but is it really? There are numerous situations in which it might actually be possible to release a product of intentionally lower quality than you would otherwise produce.

I don't mean missing a few features (that would be reducing C). I mean releasing some of the included content before it's 100 percent right. Maybe it's more important to capture a particular market window and you know that your customers would be reasonably tolerant of a few flaws. Of course, you're certainly not going to allow quality issues that could be truly life-threatening or make your product completely unusable. But there are probably a few areas that could stand a few hiccups and still result in a successful venture overall. It's a calculated risk, but the key word there is *calculated*. By using the formula, you can remind yourself to at least ask about the possibility of reducing quality.

Now, getting everyone to agree that the project scope can change is one thing. But be sure to make it clear to both your managers and your team that nobody is going to try to force through a change that is simply beyond the ability of the team to complete. Nothing will destroy your carefully built motivation faster than a task that is simply impossible. You have to stay within reasonable parameters when you add or change the total size of the project.

The basic *CQBS* equation has to remain about the same. But as long as it does, you'll be staying within the basic boundaries of the initial goal and producing a better product than your initial plan.

Let's return to the common situation in which your estimated project schedule (*S*) is simply too large for the powers that be. Using the formula, what options do we have if we wish to decrease *S*?

- We can increase the neighboring value (B): We need more run-rate budget. Can we have more people? Can we have more dollars applied to other support needs?
- We can decrease the size of the product (C): What can be removed? What can we simplify?
- We can decrease the quality of our content (Q): As mentioned above, it may be acceptable to finish the product and still have a few problems unresolved.

Now, when the Big Boss asks if you can get something done sooner, or if you can build more into your product, you don't have to immediately jump to the standard "If you want it sooner, I need more people" response. Instead, you can trade off content, quality, budget, and schedule all day long.

When you're estimating, always look back at the formula to give yourself clues about what you can adjust. Even though you'd be wise to expect pushback on any schedule you propose, there's no reason not to consider all the variables even before you submit your first estimate and shuffle priorities based on constraints you may already know about. If you know that the deadline is going to be truly inflexible, for example, look at the other variables and see what you can propose at the very start. Ask if you can request additional resources or if a "light" first implementation would be possible. Be proactive and see what happens.

Tweaking the Numbers

When you are backed into a corner, and the upper management group is trying to lock in all of those *CQBS* variables, the difference between what they're asking for and what you know your team is able to accomplish might be huge. On the other hand, the difference might be small enough that, given just a few more resources, you might be able to pull this one off.

Of course, the first demand will be that you simply tell your team to work longer and get the job done. And depending on the particular situation, that might be enough to be successful. However, if your people just got done with an overwork situation, they won't be very happy jumping into another one, and then another one after that. To avoid crushing morale and motivation—in which case you'll have no chance at success whatsoever—you need to come up with a different plan.

Instead, you can push back. You can lay out the situation and show how close your team is to being fully stocked for success. Now is the time to ask for what you need: a tiny bit less content (C), an extra person or two (B), or a little extra time in the schedule (S). Something that has always amazed me is that, in more instances than not, the difference between a fatally flawed project and one with a reasonable chance of success is a lot less than you might think. Many times, you can make the undoable look doable simply by adding an extra person or an extra week or two at the end of the schedule.

When you are within tweaking range, the most powerful variable you have to play with is usually B. If you actually assign values and measure monetary costs, you will often discover that a 10 or 20 percent increase in funding levels can easily make the difference. If you firmly believe that you are close, and that a minor budget increase can radically improve your chance of success, you are obligated to make that case. Would your company really spend a million bucks on a project that could fail when they could spend 1.1 million and get something that will lead to real profit? Push for what you know is right.

Defending Your Resources

The formula even has value beyond estimating: you can use it to defend resources on a project that's already under way. If the Big Boss wants to reduce the resources you have assigned to the project, it's fair for you to ask, "What is coming out of the product?" or "Do we get more time to finish?" or "Is it okay if we skimp a little on quality now?" If the answers to these three questions are "Nothing," "No," and "No," your own management is basically telling you that your team has limitless capacity. Apparently, you previously had far too many people working on the project, or you vastly overestimated the work—because your management is now claiming that they can subtract people from the effort, but you can still bring it in on time, with all features as planned, without reducing quality one bit.

That's the time for you to push back and give them a reality check. When this has happened to me, I have asked outright, "So I guess you think we've been slacking up until now?" Sometimes putting it back on them like that—maybe a little more politely, if necessary—can provide a needed wake-up call. Then, when you're able to really sit down and negotiate some changes, you can work with your superiors to make the *CQBS* trade-off that works best for all parties.

Chapter 8: Maximizing Productivity

In the previous chapter, we discussed basic estimating and how you can work with the *CQBS* variables to produce the best possible outcome when one or more of those variables is constrained. In that discussion, *CQ* and *BS* were required to remain in proportion to each other, as dictated by the constant *k*.

$$\frac{CQ}{BS} = k$$

Recall that I defined *k* as a constant value for your organization, team, or project. But there's an inherent problem there: as long as *k* is fixed to a particular value, our ability to play with the other variables is severely constrained.

If only we could find a way to increase *k*!

But What Is This "k" Thing? Productivity!

Increase *k*? Is *k* not truly a constant? Of course not. If *k* was one unchangeable value, for all companies, under all circumstances, everywhere in the world, that would exclude the possibility that some groups could work more efficiently than others. Obviously, that doesn't make sense. k itself is a variable, and indeed, whatever the heck k turns out to be is a pretty good indicator of your team's capability. And if you could compare two teams side by side and somehow compute their k values, the team scoring higher would have a demonstrable ability to get more done, with higher quality, using fewer people over less time.

What this means is that k actually corresponds to some measure of productivity. Stated another way, your team's productivity (k) can be thought of as the ratio of what you get out of the project—content (C) and quality (Q)—to what you put into it—time (S) and money (B).

Increasing k, and Doing More with Less

Now we're getting somewhere! With this new understanding of k, we can start discussing how we might be able to actually get more done—even with less at our disposal. Instead of trading off between the *CQBS* variables on the left side of the equation, we can consider what changes we might make to our team's productivity. It's in the formula, and it's common sense. If we can improve productivity, we can get more good-quality features done. And we'll use fewer people and less time in the process.

Productivity (k) and Performance (P)

Think back to our discussion of motivation in the chapter "Working with the Team." Back then, I stated that a worker's motivation was the strongest component in determining his overall performance, which is also affected by his ability and tools:

Shutting Up

$$P = M^2AT$$

Now let's make the jump from performance on a personal level (*P*) to productivity on a team level (*k*). Logically, *k* is essentially the team equivalent of *P*:

$$P = k$$

And then we can do some substitution in our formula. The original formula

$$\frac{CQ}{BS} = k$$

Becomes

$$\frac{CQ}{BS} = P$$

Finally, substitute the variables that comprise *P*:

$$\frac{CQ}{BS} = M^2AT$$

Bumping Up Your Productivity

As I said at the beginning of this chapter, if we *really* want to improve our overall capabilities, juggling the *CQBS* variables on the left side of the equation isn't going to get us there. Instead, we should concentrate on increasing k, which we've now shown is equivalent to the items on the right side of the equation—the ones that affect performance and productivity. In other words, we should concentrate on motivation, ability, and tools.

That means, as a creative manager, you can now start asking powerful questions from several new points of view.

- Motivation: "I need to get more out of my team than ever before. How can I motivate them for this project? Can I rev them up? Can I get my boss to approve some sort of project bonus? Can I put someone in charge of this who's desperately trying to prove what he can do?"
- Ability: "Do I have the right people for the job? Maybe I could get the job done sooner and better with the same number of people if they had different skill sets. Maybe I should farm out some of this to another group or company that has the correct skills already. Maybe I can bring in some focused training for my current people."
- Tools: "What else could my people use to help them work faster, better, or smarter? Could I move them together to improve communications? Do they need new computers? New bulldozers? New phones? What if I started bringing lunches in to save time? Are we making them follow some obsolete process that might as well be handcuffs and speed bumps?"

The Formula in Action

As you can see when you understand the interrelation between the many different performance (P) and productivity (k) factors, you have quite a few weapons in your arsenal to radically improve the way your team gets the job done. Even minor changes to certain individual and team factors can markedly raise your P (or k) value.

If you can adjust most of the factors in positive ways, it's possible to increase your team's overall capabilities to many times greater than where you started.

Think about it. How much more does a highly motivated worker accomplish than someone who just shows up for work each day and does the minimum? How much better does someone with exactly the right abilities and training perform than someone who is much closer to average or who has to figure things out as he goes? And how much more efficient is a team that has the right tools and processes for the job, as opposed to a team that has to work with outdated, cast-off equipment and deal with obsolete and redundant procedures?

Combine all those factors and consider the potential performance of a highly intelligent, fully trained worker, using modern tools and techniques, who is strongly motivated to get the job done, versus the performance of an average worker, who is making do with old gear, and who doesn't think his product is that important. What might the difference in output be? Double? Triple? Ten times?

If you can make that kind of change to your P and k, your team can start producing two, three, or ten times the good-quality features—in the same amount of time and for the same cost. Or, put another way, you can get the same projects done, with the same level of quality, but finish them two, three, or ten times faster or cheaper.

Advanced k: Productivity Equals Value

Given these sets of formulas, what are the units in which the k value is measured? Let's consider that for a moment. You'll have to stretch your imagination a little (and remember your high school algebra!), but the answer does lend some value to the discussion.

Recall from the first formula that

- Our C value is the amount of content we include in our product. To keep this all generic, let's say the units of C are expressed as widgets.
- Q is a measure of the quality of each part of the delivered content. So let's express Q as quality per widget.
- Our B value is the budget available over any given period, or money per time.
- Finally, S is a straightforward measure of time.

Let's substitute each of these units into our *CQBS* equation and see what that looks like. (Remember that "x per y" can be expressed mathematically as the fraction x/y.)

Recall the original equation:

$$\frac{CQ}{BS} = k$$

Swapping out the variables with the units we just described, it becomes

$$\frac{widgets \times \frac{quality}{widget}}{\frac{money}{time} \times time} = k$$

Doing some simple algebraic cancellation, we arrive at

$$\frac{quality}{money} = k$$

Here's where we need to make a bit of a stretch, but it's a logical one. In this new equation, imagine that the idea of "quality" is a bit different from before. The initial equations represent the quality of *each individual widget*—quality per widget. But in the final equation, it's better to think of quality as *the total quality as viewed by the customer.*

This idea of "total quality" from the customer's point of view has two components: "how much stuff I get" and "how good the stuff is." Those two factors ultimately drive customer perception of overall quality. If you deliver a ton of features, and they all happen to be lousy, that's not total quality. Nor is delivering only one or two features that work very well.

Customers want it all, and they want it working well. (Wouldn't you?) And, leading in to a final set of equations, *they don't want to overpay for it.* Nobody minds paying a reasonable price for something he needs. But all else being equal, a lower price is always better. In fact, the more good stuff (total quality) that we can get for a lower price, the more value we perceive. Value *is* getting more for less, and it can be mathematically expressed as total quality per the price the customer pays:

$$\frac{quality}{price} = value$$

Now, look at the similarity between those last two equations: one uses "quality per money" (the money you invested in the product), and the other uses "quality per price" (the price the customer pays). In the first equation, money is your cost of development. In the second, price is what the customer pays. But aren't those two items pretty closely related? The less you spend to develop a product, the less you need to charge your customers to make a profit.

So if

$$\frac{quality}{price} = value$$

and

$$\frac{quality}{money} = k$$

and if the customer's price is essentially equivalent to the money you invest in development, then

$$value = k$$

So what does this mean? It means *the actual value that you provide to your customers is directly related to your team's productivity.*

Now, how powerful is *that* knowledge? If you double your k (or P) factor—no matter how you do it, whether it's through higher motivation, enhanced worker ability, or better tool availability—it provides a direct doubling of the value that your customers will perceive.

Wow.

Chapter 9: GOOOOAAAALLLL!!!!

Unlike the estimates that we discussed previously—objective guesses of time, money, or both that you use for project planning—a goal is a more subjective statement of some work to be performed. Goals for your organization might be to complete a project according to some basic parameters, change a process, or perform a reorganization.

In most organizations, goals are closely aligned with the performance reviews that we discussed in the chapter "Managing Performance." Let's dive deeper into how you can write, plan, and execute goals in your own organization.

Shared Commitment to the Goal

When you set goals for yourself and your team, whether they're written in a project plan or statements to your higher-ups, they aren't simply things that would be nice to accomplish if you can. Goals are commitments: once you make them, you live or die by your effort.

Early in my management career, I was called into a meeting with the CEO of my company. My team was just starting a new project that was vital to the company's future, and the CEO didn't know much about me yet. He stressed how critical it was that the project succeed, and he asked me if my team was going to come through for the company. I replied with "We're going to do our best on this!"

Naturally, his response was to reiterate the criticality of the project and state that our best "wasn't good enough." We *had* to come through. I realized that he and I had a totally different take on what I meant by "do our best." I clarified:

> "Oh, I agree! What I meant was we're not going to go at this half-assed and just hope to get something out the door in time. We're going to kill ourselves to finish it early and under budget for you. We're going to make you proud."

I just made a heck of a commitment, didn't I? I told the Big Boss that my team and I were "going to kill ourselves" on that big project. I committed my team along with myself. I committed that they were committed to me.

Now, do you think my team made the commitment to me before or after I made that comment to the CEO? If you said "after," welcome to Dingus land. When you drop a major commitment like that in the team's lap after you've made it to the higher-ups, you are guaranteed to fail. It is critical that the team determine what they are able to do and commit to you before you go making promises to anyone else. Get the team behind you first. Then you can go on to make outlandish statements to the CEO.

Writing Goals

The first step in writing solid goals is, obviously, to figure out roughly what the goals should be. In general, goals that are tied to the completion of projects will be the most useful. Projects are what make money, and the use of project goals leaves you with the freedom to make other changes, as needed, in support of that objective.

For example, imagine that you write two different goals: one is to complete a project, and the other is to overhaul a specific process. What happens when you find that the two goals are in conflict with each other? What if the project-management team determines that the most efficient way to complete the project requires you to leave that particular process alone, or to change it in some way other than you specified in the goal? The overall project is what's important, not so much how you get there. Leave it to the team to deal with their own processes and tools.

On to this year's goals. We know the big projects we'll be working on. But we don't have the exact requirements yet, much less any estimates for how long the work will actually take. How do we handle it?

Make Them Broad …

Recognize that the specifics don't matter. Especially if you work in an environment in which requirements can continually change during the project execution, overly specific goals will most likely never get done. Once the project is under way, somebody will change something that causes the work to diverge from that overly specific goal. What do you do now? Rewrite everyone's goal sheets to match? Okay, then how often do you have to update to keep everyone's work and goals in sync? Monthly? Weekly? What a hassle! Sure, you could leave the goals alone instead, but now your people are working toward goals that don't really exist. Is that somehow better than simply not having goals at all?

When you write your goals, don't sweat the small stuff. Cover the basics, and leave the specifics out. Written properly, goals should clarify the intent and major parameters of the project. The unwritten details will be filled in as the project progresses. That doesn't make them bad goals; it makes them realistic ones.

Take this example:

> "Complete version 3 of the XXXX product, with major business value features included, no later than the end of the third quarter, requiring no major corrections by the end of the year."

Yes, that's written fairly loosely. We don't know what the "major business value features" are yet. Even if we did, we might change one or more of them before the project is actually completed—maybe adjusting for customer demand (and hopefully an accompanying increase in revenue) or because you need to rebalance the *CQBS* variables we discussed in the previous chapter. We don't want to impede change simply because our goals were written too strictly. But we don't want to have to go rewrite them, either.

... But Not Too Broad

Goals should be broad, but that doesn't mean "enormous." If you can split your goals into a few smaller, bite-size pieces, that's preferable to one Big Bang goal. Always try to break a big parent task down into several individual phases. These intermediate milestones will allow greater clarity for your workers and make it easier to keep track of how far you've gotten. And, as each milestone is completed, you will have more opportunities to celebrate success.

However, don't fall into the trap of creating goals that can be measured only subjectively. As much as possible, all milestones need to be absolutely demonstrable: either you can see it or you can't. A goal like "Be 50 percent complete with development" is a farce. How do you measure "completeness"? You'll never get anyone to agree. And that usually means that the goal will be marked as completed by default, because you won't want to spoil someone's day with a failing grade that he can reasonably argue is not deserved.

Keep it objective enough that anyone can make the call. Demonstrable goals and milestones drive real performance and progress.

Make Them Consistent

Once you have created the list of major goals for the year, they should be adopted downward throughout your organization. In this way, the goals for each of your managers, and for their own people, will directly support your own goals. Each worker who has responsibility for any portion of one of the top goals should have that goal included in his own goals for the year—verbatim.

When goals are the same for everyone who's contributing to a project, it has a big positive effect on teamwork and collaboration. You're sending your team the message that it isn't enough to be successful only at their own individual jobs; the whole project must succeed. Each person will, of course, have a particular area of expertise. But the project-level goal will entice your workers to help out on tasks that fall a little outside their own direct responsibilities. When everyone wins or loses as a team, your workers will be willing to do whatever is necessary to make that goal happen.

On a similar note, if you have your own direct management team, you can send an even stronger message to them. They should each have every one of your personal goals as one of their own, *even if their particular team is not involved in all of those goals*. This will force your managers to play together better, help out whenever they can, and generally not play politics with each other over their people and resources. If you have the ability to weight goals, it's OK to adjust the relative weights of each goal to compensate for those items that they truly have (or don't have) within their scope of control. Just don't take any of the weights all the way down to zero. Again, they all win or lose together.

Press a Little

Don't be afraid to press when you lay out goals for your team. Although we managers might sometimes think so, we are not omniscient. If we don't know how to accomplish something, that doesn't mean that nobody knows. And just because you think something is impossible doesn't necessarily make it so. You want to encourage your team to find a way.

Entrepreneurial leaders are the kings of the press-goal technique. "I need this completely new product developed in two weeks." You, personally, might think it's not doable in that time frame, but maybe you've got a creative genius who can dream up a totally new way to get across the finish line in world-record time. For him it could be old hat, and that two weeks could be twice as much time as he needs to make it happen.

I'm not advocating impossible goals, but it's okay to give the team a challenge. They will push back as much as they need to until you can all find a happy medium.

Get Them Done ...

As the goals become due, don't give credit for anything less than absolute completion. Goals are not *almost*; they are *done*. When you start saying "good enough" at *almost done*, or *nearly done*, soon your people will be expecting it at *mostly done* or *kind of done* ... or even lower. Stick to the goal!

"Did you finish that task?"

"Yep, all done! All that's left is ..."

Shutting Up

"Whoa! Something's left? Is it *totally* done or not?"

"Well ... no, I guess not."

By the way, this may be a good time to mention the "95 percent principle." For some reason, many projects at the 95 percent point have a way of taking about 30 percent more time to cover that final 5 percent of the project. That's one more reason to require that *done means done.*

... But Avoid Ridiculousness

Didn't I just say that "done means done," period? Okay, so there's an exception to that rule, but "almost done" isn't it. It's when valid extenuating circumstances really are involved, and not recognizing them would just make you a Dingus.

Early in my career, before I entered the management lair, I was asked by the executive staff to take on a critical project. I was one of the very few people in the company who happened to have the needed skill set. I made it clear that this would bump other work off my plate, and their response was "Nothing is more important than this." My boss and I rearranged things, and I spent the next two months blasting away at the new project. I was successful, and there were hearty pats on the back all around.

At the end of the year, my manager carefully wrote up my performance review. He included several reminders of that project I had completed for the executive staff earlier in the year. But when the review came back, I had been downgraded. I hadn't completed all the work laid out in my goals—the goals that the urgent project had bumped, with the full advance knowledge of the executive team. No credit was given for the critical project, either.

What? The goals were not modifiable during the year, so we couldn't have changed them. My manager sent his questions back to the executive staff, and he was answered with "We really appreciate that Eric came through on that, but we have to grade everyone purely on the basis of the work assigned in the goals." Can you guess what kind of message that sent to me and everyone else who heard the story?

Moral of the story? If I had known that's how it was going to turn out, I should have done one of the following:

- Demanded modification to my goals before I did the work (and probably been fired).
- Told them that the goals were the goals, that's what I was going to work on, the critical project could wait, even if it brought the company down, and thank you very much (and probably been fired).
- Departed and gone to work for a company that respected its people and provided flexibility (and told the executive staff that they had mud for brains—and probably been fired in absentia).

Better moral? Remember that setting people to work on the right projects at the right time is what makes you and your company successful. Don't penalize people for doing the right thing. Be flexible. And if it's one of *your* workers in that situation, you'd better defend him to the hilt—right up to turning in your own resignation.

Rewarding Properly

When it comes to merit increases and project bonuses, being a manager is a pretty tricky job. You know what *you* think is right. But then you're going to have to sync that up with what everyone else in management wants to do, not to mention whatever constraints are placed on you from the top-level bosses or the HR department. Only in the rarest of circumstances—like when you run your own company with nobody else to placate—will it come out as well as you'd probably like. But let's see what we can do.

Dealing with Human Resources and Management

It's always a good idea to cultivate a friendly relationship with your Human Resources group. (See the chapter "Beyond the Team" at the end of the book.) When you know how you want to reward your people, it's time to use that relationship to try to bend whatever rules you might need to.

Of course, no matter how good the relationship you develop, sometimes the HR team is completely constrained by rules from above. Their freedom of action is usually inversely proportional to the size of the company. Small-company HR can usually create, bend, and break the rules. But big corporate HR teams might as well try to strike the letter Z from the alphabet.

One of the greatest challenges I've had with merit increases and bonuses for my team is the tendency of larger companies to "level the playing field." They operate as if every worker is capable of the same quantity and quality of work, and they employ compensation, merit increase, and bonus systems that provide very little incentive for workers to truly excel. Unfortunately, typical merit increase systems too often award the average employee something like a 2 percent salary increase, while the top employees get 3 percent and the lowest ones on the totem pole get only 1 percent.

Wow, what a range! How sad. Differentials like this only encourage everyone to move to the center of the performance curve, and for the bottom group it probably won't do even that. Your top people will think, *It doesn't matter if I really excel. The extra few bucks in my raise don't add up to anything.* Granted, we've discussed that money is not usually a worker's primary motivating factor. And yes, you have other tools to use: praise, better assignments, promotions. But if the reward tool is there, why not use it as intended? If you're going to bother with merit increases or bonuses at all, why not give them appropriately, based on each individual's true contributions?

Work as much as needed with your HR department and upper management team to sculpt a set of policies that announce to everyone, "Our top people are the keys to our future success. We must make it impossible for them to be unhappy over something as simple as compensation." HR or management may feel that an extra percent over what the "average" workers are getting is sufficient to get that message across, so it's your job to make them understand how false that belief really is.

I actually had one HR leader tell me that his team liked to keep things egalitarian so that managers wouldn't use "favoritism" as a mechanism for determining increases. Huh? I absolutely want my favorite workers to get the biggest increases! Of course, when I say *favorite*, I mean "this person will almost kill himself to get his work done and always does a fantastic job." If the HR leader meant "the person I like going to lunch with or my longtime friend," then you have a completely different problem in need of a solution.

Playing Favorites

Playing favorites is just fine—as long as you base your favoritism on each worker's P score in the $P=M^2AT$ equation, and nothing else. Remember that a worker's performance comes from high motivation, high ability, and the quality of the tools that he brings to the table (when applicable). Performance leads to more $CQBS$ for you, and that leads to more profits.

Take the top 10 to 20 percent of your workers, and do everything within your power to treat them excessively well. Those people are your livelihood. If 3 percent increases are this year's norm, then your topmost workers may deserve 6 percent or more. If this year's bonus standard is to award most people 10 percent of their salaries, your best employees should be getting 20 percent or more.

In fact, why does anyone not in the top 20 to 40 percent of all players deserve any bonus at all? A bonus should reward work performed beyond the call of duty. A bonus should be reserved for the people who drag everyone else in your organization across the finish line. Bonuses should be for the people whom everyone else aspires to be, and with whom everyone else wants to work.

So pool up the bonus money and award it only to your top performers. The rest of your team will know how much work that group did anyway, and they'll be happy that the top people are being incented to stick around and help them be better at what they themselves do. And maybe that hefty check will help incent other people to get themselves up to the bonus level, too.

Thinking Outside the "Bonus Box"

When your options for financial rewards are limited, be creative about finding other ways to give your top people an extra pat on the back. Some of the options might overlap with some of the motivating factors we discussed earlier. In fact, you could find yourself creating a vicious cycle of motivation: good rewards increase motivation, which increases performance, which earns more rewards. Have fun with it.

There's one unusual perk that I have found can serve as a valuable bonus: sending your best performers to an industry conference or training event. Yep, I used the word *bonus* for this. Think about it. The actual value that's gleaned from conferences and industry events is usually pretty minimal. If it's current news, information, and best practices you want, online feeds and forums are probably much more up to date. If you're looking for training, there are books and online learning out the wazoo. And all of that can be obtained right in the office at minimal or no cost.

The real benefit of attendance, at most events, is in the rubbing of elbows with people from other parts of the industry. These events are about making connections, and the people you send should feel appreciated that you felt good enough about them to spend thousands of dollars on their travel and attendance. Reserve that kind of treatment only for your top players, solely as an additional reward.

Chapter 10: Maintaining Perspective

Throughout the early chapters of this book, I alluded to a number of situations in which it's important to maintain perspective. When one of your workers makes a mistake, for example, remember that unless you're operating a nuclear missile silo, an honest mistake is unlikely to result in the actual end of the world. Now, let's discuss a few more examples of the value of perspective.

Keeping the Small-Company Perspective

If you have ever worked for a very large company, undoubtedly that corporation has a few policies and procedures in place that drive you (and most everyone around you) absolutely nuts. When you're filling out form 8467b(1) in triplicate to requisition a stapler, you can't help but wonder, *How the heck did anyone ever come up with this?* Small start-ups never seem to have these problems. So what happened?

What Were They Thinking?

I encountered one of my personal favorite policies at the company where I worked a few years ago. Our expense reimbursement system was spectacularly manual. In addition to the hard-copy forms we had to complete, we were required to tape all of our receipts to a sheet of paper and mail (not email) the whole package to a processing center. When the finance group announced that this process was going to be automated, there was rejoicing throughout the land. Everyone was using company credit cards anyway, so it seemed logical that the information could be captured electronically to radically modernize the system.

You have probably guessed that it didn't turn out that way. We now had an online form to complete. Granted, that was much better than writing it down and adding it all up manually. And now we could scan our receipts and attach them electronically to the submission. Great!

But a couple of weeks after I submitted my first claim, I received an email indicating that the processing team still hadn't received my receipts. Of course, I responded that I had submitted them electronically along with the expense form. "Yes, but we still require the hard copies of the original receipts to be mailed in."

I responded, "Oh, so we don't have to scan them?"

"Yes, we need both."

Cue me bouncing my skull off my desk. Repeatedly.

This wonderful new process was developed by someone in finance and approved by the CFO without much thought or cross-checking with other teams. It didn't matter that everyone in the company was now committed to a bunch of extra work. The process seemed correct to whoever thought it up, and that's all that mattered.

At another company, my direct boss was required to approve every new hire I was going to make—even though I controlled my own budget for the year, and even if the hire was simply a replacement for someone we'd lost. My boss had to sign off anyway. So what's so bad about that? Well, it wasn't only my direct boss who needed to approve. It was also my boss's boss (I call this person my "two-boss"). And just in case that doesn't sound quite heavyweight enough, the same boss and two-boss also had to sign off on the job posting to open the position in the first place. Not only did that waste everyone's time, it was a sideways acknowledgment that I wasn't really in control even of my own team. The company was telling me, "We don't really trust you to make decisions, even those within your budgetary scope."

So What's My Point?

Most of these large companies presumably started as small companies long ago—maybe even as start-ups. If you've been part of a start-up or small company, you know that things are optimized for action. There's real work to do, and there isn't enough time in the day to do it, much less to waste it on pointless or redundant processes. So as those companies grew from start-up size to their current bulky glory, how and why did they allow themselves to degenerate so many of their processes and procedures into heavyweight, burdensome, and confusing piles of garbage? When a process change was proposed, didn't someone examine the costs and benefits to ensure that the change would truly result in an improvement?

For every crappy process you have to deal with, somebody once put it into place ... on purpose. Who was there at that time, why did they do it, and why didn't anyone call them out on it? Sure, it might have been the CEO, but even he can be bargained with (usually). And it probably wasn't the top dog—it was more likely a new hire in some service-oriented department, trying to make his mark or duplicate what he saw his last boss do at another large company.

Stick with What Works

Learn from this. If your company is small but growing, watch for the warning signs and try to avoid the pitfalls. When you bring in new people to support the growth and shore up your service departments, try to hire people who will institute processes and procedures that have been properly molded to fit your company's particular situation. Don't bring in people who want to implement "big company" processes just because that's what they happen to have experience with.

Even if the company is already large, why limit yourself to such predictably high-overhead processes? Look at your processes and ask whether an efficient start-up would handle them the same way. Simpler is better. Do you really need to sign off on in-budget hires for replacements four levels below you?

While you're at it, ask your team which processes they hate and what they feel could be easily optimized, whether those processes are inside or outside your scope of control. They'll tell you. If it's within your ability to change it, do it. If not, muster up as much support as you can get from your peers and negotiate a change with the controlling department.

And as for you: when you make process changes, make sure you're doing the right thing for the right reasons. Don't add useless processes because you think that's how successful companies do it. Stick with what really works.

Keeping Problems in Proportion

Why does it seem that we always have so many big problems to deal with? You'd think there would come a point when all of those major issues have been dealt with and we can relax—just a little. But they keep on coming, and on any given day our list of problems looks just as long as before.

Over the short term, that certainly may be true. No matter how well you handle them, big problems take time to resolve. But let's consider what really happens over a longer period of time—say, a year. (The ideal time period varies by the industry, your team, and the types of projects you handle. If you've been brought in to clean up an area or a product, it could be longer. That's probably why your area needed cleanup in the first place.) Of course, this exercise assumes that your basic job and responsibilities are about the same as they were last year.

First, create a list of your biggest issues from a year ago. Use email trails, notebooks you keep, old status reports, and so on to generate the best record you can. Then put together your list of current issues. On each list, assign each item a severity level of "big," "medium," or "small."

Now, compare the two sets of issues. If you've been working to improve your people, improve communications, update inefficient processes, and generally help your team be more productive, you may find that the average level of severity is a little less dire right now. Surprised?

Sure, you still have problems to deal with. You always will. And, from your immediate perspective, you still have big problems that need to be fixed. But when you compare those two lists, you might find that items you currently consider "big" would have made only the "medium" category a year ago. It's just that after you solve all your bigger problems, your smaller problems *become* your bigger ones. You have to step back, look at the issues that you and your team are contending with, and realize that things might actually be getting better overall.

When I've done this exercise with my teams, we've actually looked at each other in amazement and said things like "Wow, these are the things we consider to be our biggest problems now?" Getting that fresh perspective is important for both your own well-being and your team's. Again, there will always be problems, but it's both gratifying and vital to recognize the improvement that you've made. Plus, making people feel good about their accomplishments is a powerful way to provide motivation to continue the effort.

More importantly, you have to recognize your own successes. It's great if you have a boss who showers you with praise for your wins more frequently than your annual performance review. But, let's face it, that can be rare. And you probably beat yourself up enough over the things that go wrong. So take some time periodically to look at what you've done right, and pat yourself on the back. Not just for those short-term successes that are easy to track—use this exercise to track the long-term effects of your efforts as well. And when you can look at your own set of "big" problems and chuckle to yourself, "Wow, these are the worst problems I have?" you'll sleep much better that night.

Chapter 11: Getting Respect

Despite what Machiavelli may have written, as a good, team-oriented manager you can't achieve your own personal goals while leaving a continuous stream of disasters in your wake. The ends do not justify the means, and no one with any self-respect wants to be seen as the world's biggest Dingus. True self-respect goes hand in hand with respect from your team and peers.

Let's discuss some techniques we can use to build up a higher level of respect from your compatriots. There may be multiple paths to success, but the techniques we'll discuss here will get you there with everyone respecting who you are and how you achieved those results.

Let Your Team Find Solutions

As the boss, do you make that extra five cents per hour because of your ability to belch forth wonderful answers to anyone's questions? Nope. Is it because you can come to a flawless decision in every situation based only on your many years of experience, without the need for assistance or consultation? Nah. Perhaps because you issue brilliant orders with no concern for context or circumstances? No way.

Maybe it's because you facilitate while the team coordinates itself, allowing your people to gather relevant information and assimilate everything into a suitable course forward, and trying to stay out of everyone's way as much as you can. There you go!

Throughout your career, you will encounter managers who will insist that it is the manager's job to make decisions in a vacuum. I know I've worked with them. It's sort of amazing to watch this ego at work. He's more interested in seeing his favorite thoughts translated into reality than in seeing the right ideas implemented. Because this kind of decision-making approach usually leads down a sad path, managers like this oftentimes become adept at exercising selective amnesia about who exactly thought up the idea in the first place. But strangely, they have no such problem when their decisions happen to lead to a rare success.

The best managers lead their teams by helping their team members to execute properly. For you as that manager, a good chunk of your job comes down to trust. Do you trust your team to make the tough decisions?

Of course you can be involved. You certainly need to intervene when they decide to do something downright nutsy or dangerous! But dictating your team's every move won't do much for building up their confidence or allowing them to grow. Be willing to let them branch out on their own every once in a while. And be willing to let them make some mistakes on their own. (Remember Tell, Sell, and Solo? It applies to teams, too.) If your team can learn something from a less-than-fully-successful attempt, and the organization can absorb the lost time, the long-term effect of their experiment can be well worth it. Teach your team to fish for their own answers rather than handing them a freshly filleted solution every time.

Remember, too, that not everything you consider impossible necessarily must be. You can ask clarifying questions to ensure that the team has considered all the information they need to come to a solid decision. If you get answers you didn't expect, or answers you don't like, you can try rewording your questions if necessary. But don't be surprised if the sum total of the other brains outweighs yours. Be prepared to swallow the fact that you can be wrong from time to time, and if your team's argument is reasonable, let them go down the path of their own choosing. Especially if they know you have some doubts, they will stop at nothing to make it work and prove they were right. Ownership is a beautiful thing.

By the way, the reverse is also true. If you try to jam something down the team's throat, they might feel compelled to try to make it happen, especially if they have no real opinion of their own. But even if your idea is the best one, if they already have a distaste for it, some of them will make sure it fails—even if it's only subconsciously. Better to be wrong yourself and have it all turn out right in the end.

Take Responsibility

It's very easy to take the kudos when things have gone well, isn't it? But what about when you seriously screw up? It happens. And when it does, admit it. Acknowledge the error and take full responsibility. Don't try to downplay it, and don't try to cover it up. We all know that cover-ups don't work anyway—someone always finds out. And when that happens, the ensuing scandal will completely blow whatever street cred you might have had.

Taking It for the Team

After you've accepted your share of the responsibility, go one better: try to grab other people's share too. This is especially crucial when one of your people has underperformed, or if your whole team has messed something up. When that happens, it's imperative that you take full responsibility and not attempt to deflect any blame onto the team. The people on your team will really appreciate that you shouldered some of the fallout, and it makes them even more likely to go to the mat for you next time.

So what happens to you, then? Will you be chastised and demoted? Unlikely. Despite your attempts to swallow the majority of the blame, most people will know that the screwup was not entirely your fault. Your attempt to attract more ire than you're due will most likely result in less unpleasantness for you, rather than more, as your managers and peers recognize and respect your actions.

Handling Unhappy Customers

It's especially critical to take responsibility when you're dealing with unhappy customers. Have you ever watched someone handle a situation with comments like "It's not really as bad as you think it is" or "That's not our fault," while the customer just gets madder and madder? I assure you, your customers aren't interested in hearing excuses like that. When I speak with unhappy customers, I always begin with something like this:

> "Thanks for letting me speak with you today. I first want to say that I know sometimes it feels like we're some faceless blob and that maybe your problems aren't getting our attention. Sales and service are telling you that we're working on things, but I understand you think they could be just trying to calm you down. But I assure you, we know what your problems are. Our sales and service team have kept us completely up to date on your situation, and we're going to make this work. We're working on these problems with much more vigor than a forty-hour workweek, and we are committed to getting things right.

"We are very unhappy with ourselves that this has happened. We take real pride in our work, and nobody wants this fixed more than I do. This is not up to my standards, it is totally my responsibility, and I apologize for the pain you've been having."

That is how you get a customer's respect.

Note that this works even if some of the problems the customer is having aren't really in your area. That's because the customer doesn't care about your company's internal organization. He wants to know that someone there is looking out for him. If you say, "This item is someone else's problem, you'll have to try to talk to them," you're passing the buck and letting the customer know that his problems may never be solved.

If a customer's problem is truly out of your control, it's okay to say something like "That item isn't in our area, but we will take responsibility for getting the word through to the right people." Let the customer know that, even though it isn't really your problem, you're going to *make* it your problem until it gets fixed. Take the bull by the horns, swallow your pride if you need to, and give the customer what he needs.

Be Positively Predictable

Predictable? I know, that sounds pretty boring. But remember, we aren't talking about social relationships here. We're discussing how to achieve results at work. And at work, there's nothing I appreciate more than someone whose predictability can bore me to tears. When someone is predictable, it means I understand him. I know exactly what to expect from him—both how he performs and how he acts.

Of course, predictability isn't such a good thing when someone predictably fails to perform or act appropriately. Let's take a closer look.

Performance

Clearly, the more important of these is performance. When you have someone you can absolutely count on to perform excellently all the time, you know you can rely on him to get the job done. You don't have to worry about whether he's actually "on" the problem or not. He's got it. Let him be.

By extension, the same is true when others look at you. Do you perform with excellence every time? When your team or boss needs something, do you come through consistently? When you make a commitment, can they absolutely count on you fulfilling it?

I've worked with too many people who never came even close to landing in the consistency ballpark. The Big Boss would ask them for the same thing multiple times, showing an increasing level of displeasure at each request, and they still couldn't come through. That kind of performance can become predictable too, but not in a way that's going to move you very quickly up the ladder. And if you're unreliable about commitments you make to your team members, it won't take long for you to lose all credibility and respect with them either.

Once you've made a commitment, consider yourself committed. You must follow through and perform to your utmost on every commitment you make, no matter how far out of your way you have to go. So if you're in a position where you can't actually commit, don't! Explain what you can do, and make that your commitment instead. Ultimately, people will appreciate your honesty and feel confident that you'll keep your promises and follow through on your commitments.

Action

Predictability in action is also crucial. As a manager, you want to know that every person on your team will handle himself appropriately in any given situation. If you send a worker out to visit a customer, you want to know that he will treat the customer properly, even if the customer begins to get agitated. As with performance, your confidence in someone's predictable action comes from repeated exposure. When you've already seen that worker handle tough customers many times, you can be confident that he'll do it right this time too.

Now, turn it around again and think about how others view you. When someone alerts you to some impending disaster, are you the Dingus that shoots the messenger? Do you start screaming and running around the room? Do you start firing off commands to try to fix things before you have a true understanding of the problem? If those are your predictable actions, you need to reexamine them.

Your team needs you to be as predictable—*positively* predictable—as you want them to be. They need you to remain calm, cool, and collected. They need you to ask the right questions, collect the appropriate data, and provide real leadership toward a solution. Never forget that you are the captain of the ship. Act like it.

Follow the Rules

Your company has rules. Your boss has rules. You probably have some personal rules of your own. You preach the importance of compliance to your whole team. You expect the rules to be followed.

But then you're at a business dinner with a few of your team members. Normal company policy in this situation requires the highest-ranking person to pay for the meal and submit the expense to his boss for reimbursement. Instead, you let one of your subordinates pick up the check. That way, *you* can sign off on the expense report without passing it up to your boss. No big deal—you know your boss won't have a problem with the expense. It's just easier if you don't have to bother sending it up the line. Right?

Not quite. What message did you just send to your subordinates? You clearly demonstrated that you're willing to circumvent the rules when it's convenient for you. What other rules are you willing to bend or break? Do you want your people doing the same thing?

It's amazing how easy it is to send the wrong signal. At least that dinner check pass-the-buck was probably a violation of general company policy—someone else's rule, not one of your own. But if it was your rule, give yourself a good smack. If you can't follow the rules you make on your own, why bother?

Never expect any of your team members to follow the rules any better than you do. If there's truly room for slack in certain circumstances, be sure to make that clear. Otherwise, be the example you are supposed to be.

This most especially applies to rules of an ethical nature—both personal and business related. Finances, Human Resources, intellectual property rights, legal issues, whatever—always plainly show your commitment to maintaining clear ethical principles. And don't restrict yourself to the rules passed down from On High. Feel free to add in your own flavoring if you think a situation commands it.

Sucking It Up: Selling a Management Decision

Think back to our discussion about how you should handle issues between your group and another team that you don't command. I mentioned that when you're the one who's having a change forced down your throat, it's important for you to not let your team know your displeasure. That might seem a little counterintuitive, but let me explain.

Spinning the Positive

When you make a policy or procedural change that goes significantly counter to current thought, your team will want to know why. If you thought it through and think it's a good call, the explanation is easy. But if you're unhappy about the change, you have two choices for how to present it to your team. You can tell them you were forced into the decision and you hate it with every fiber of your being. Or you can explain why it's the best outcome and sell it as if the change was actually your choice from the very beginning. Pick one:

> "Everyone, we have to make a change to our policy of requiring that extra paperwork for service requests. Yeah, this is going to make it harder for us, and we'll probably be dealing with support problems for a long time. Just so we're clear, I didn't want this—those other teams did—and it's happening only because the Big Boss made me do it. I'm sure not going to go out of my way to give those other teams any great support on that stuff from now on."

Or

> "Everyone, I've decided to change our policy about the

extra paperwork for service requests. I've spoken with the other teams, and this will speed them up so they can get the big project done on time. It will probably make for some increase in work for us, and I'm sorry about that. But we'll all be helping the company make more money this year, and that will help everyone, including us. Let's make this work. I'd love to hear your ideas for ways we can make it happen."

In the first case, your team might respect the fact that you fought tooth and nail to defend the current policies, and you might think that will make you look stronger. But your workers will also see that you ultimately lost. What else are you going to fail to defend when the time comes? What if it's something personally important to one of your people, like his raise or promotion? That kind of mixed-bag respect doesn't help you much in the long run.

In the second case, though, your team sees you as an initiator, a negotiator, and a decision maker. You're a leader who's watching out for what's best for the company overall. Your people might not like that you're bringing a little more pain on them, but when you're doing it to further the big picture, you're helping them avoid the biggest pain of all: being out of work. Plus, you're showing that you're willing to help carry the load and get what's best for everyone, even when it isn't entirely popular—so your team can bet you'll go to the mat for them when the time comes.

That sounds like a real leader to me. And it sounds like the way to garner true respect from your team.

Be Proactive

In fact, there's a way to handle this situation even better. Instead of waiting for the bomb to drop, and dealing with it all after the decision is made, see if you can be more proactive when you first see the change coming. As soon as you realize that pressure is starting to build for you to move in a different direction, and you're not happy with the possibility, get your team involved right away. In the last example, I ended with "Let's make this work. I'd love to hear your ideas for ways we can make it happen."

But why wait until the decision is final to drop it on your team? A few days earlier, you could have said this instead:

> "We're having discussions about this situation now. We haven't decided on a final course of action yet, so I'd love to hear any of your ideas I could throw into the mix. If we do decide to go this other way, I'd like to have some good ideas for how we would adapt and make it work out well."

When you take this proactive approach, two things might happen. In the best case, your people will actually give you legitimate ammunition that supports your side, and you can swing things back your way and totally avoid the problem. Terrific! But if the change still goes through, it can only help if your people can help develop the processes to make things work.

Note, however, that nowhere in your speech did you say that you hated one of the choices. If that choice does come to be, your team will remember your words and realize that the change came over your objections. Make a habit of looking on the bright side, at least in public, and save the venting for elsewhere.

Selling It

You can announce changes the same way almost anytime that you need to pass word from above down to your people. It's part of your job as a manager: represent what has been agreed upon by the overall management team, even if it isn't the decision you wanted.

When you make the announcement, lay out the case for your team to support it as well. It's your job to defend that management decision as if it was your own original idea. Your people should absolutely believe that you proposed it, you got your way, and now you're fully committed to making it happen.

Even if you can't fully convince your team to agree with your position, they'll respect you more for your ability and strength. That's much better than leaving them with the belief that nobody ever listens to you.

Assume Nothing Stays Secret

As a manager, you deal with many items that are confidential. The company's proprietary information and future plans are one thing—anyone caught sharing that is in big trouble. But you also have access to a great deal of Human Resources information, like your team members' job grades, salaries, and bonuses, that's intended for your eyes only. So when you decide on personnel actions like salary increases and promotions for your employees, you might make the assumption that everything will stay neatly tucked under the covers. And you might believe that if you treat two similar employees in highly dissimilar ways you can get away with it as a necessary evil. Yeah, Aaron makes 25 percent less than Bob, and their jobs, skills, and performance are virtually identical … but you really don't have the budget to give Aaron a big pay boost. And Aaron will never find out anyway.

Such assumptions are both wrong and dangerous. What if your employees *do* find out? Will they appreciate the manner in which they've been treated? Most likely, no one is going to hack into your employee database, but people do talk—especially if they're friends. After enough comparing of notes, your employees will figure out the big picture.

They'll Find a Way

Many years ago, the employees at my company asked management for a description of how annual review scores were assigned and how they related to merit increases. The employees wanted to know what type of bell curve was applied to the ratings, and how someone's rating mapped into money. The company was hesitant to release this information. They wanted the ability to fudge a bit—to tell people who got the second-highest rating that "nobody ever gets the top rating," or to tell a few of the best people that "no raises were larger than yours."

So, being curious and determined, my fellow employees came up with their own plan. After each person received his rating and merit increase, he wrote the information down on a ballot-like paper and anonymously dropped it into a big box. After the submissions had been gathered, a group of workers went through the data and came up with a very clear, and eye-opening, picture of the ratings and increases. Management credibility took a big hit, and it required quite a while to recover. And the next year, the overall plan details were released to everyone at the start.

The point is, you can't assume that your people will never know where they stand compared with each other. So make sure that your relative treatment of all your employees would stand up to public scrutiny. This doesn't mean that everyone has to be paid the same. But when one person's pay is different from someone else's with the same job, the reason should be clearly explainable.

Secrets Are Not Healthy Anyway

I mentioned above that it's dangerous to assume that an underpaid employee will never find out that his salary is so unequal to that of others. What happens if Aaron, now making 25 percent less than he should, talks to his friends at other companies or starts to job shop? He's going to see huge opportunity for improvement. He may come speak with you, but why would he? He doesn't know it's just him—he now thinks your company pays everyone poorly. And asking for a raise is hard. It's much easier to simply depart for the larger paycheck at another company. Or what if he's friends with Bob and finds out about the internal disparity? He's really not going to want to stick around under a manager who would treat him so unfairly.

Either way, now you have to hire a new person from the outside—assuming your own management allows you to replace Aaron at all. You'll suffer the productivity reduction of the vacant position; deal with interviewing, hiring, and training someone new; and then have to wait patiently through the time the new employee needs to fully come up to speed. And, by the way, do you think you'll be paying that new worker anything like Aaron's salary? Or will it be closer to what Aaron should have been paid in the first place?

Put yourself in Aaron's shoes one more time. Imagine your peers at your company do the same job you do, with the same experience, with the same performance ratings. How would you feel if you found out, tomorrow, that they're all paid twice what you are? I doubt you'd think that your Dingus boss was watching out for you.

It is your job to ferociously watch out for your people. Fix the situation before it degenerates. Act as if it will become public knowledge tomorrow. Would you be confident in your ability to back up the status quo? If there's no logical reason for someone to be that far out of range, deal with it before it's out of your hands.

Negotiating Fairly

After all my years of negotiating everything from corporate

acquisitions to my kids' bedtimes, my two favorite negotiation stories are both about purchasing new cars. And they both illustrate the importance of balanced negotiations and the necessity of going for the win-win resolution.

Imbalance Is Impossible

Many years ago, I tagged along with my friend when he went to purchase a new car. We all know that negotiating for a new car is about as much fun as a paper cut on your tongue, but we pretty much know how to do it. The dealer starts with the list price, you counter with what you're willing to pay, and the salesman writes it up. Then he takes your offer to his manager, because he has no power whatsoever to bargain. You twiddle your thumbs for a while, and eventually the salesman comes back with a new price from the manager. The process continues however many rounds until you reach a deal.

So when my friend and I sat down with the salesman, and he asked my friend for his starting price, my friend said he'd be willing to pay $20,000. We waited while the salesman wrote it all up and dutifully took it to the sales manager. When he returned, we were all ready for the counteroffer. But what the salesman actually said was "Sorry, that's not high enough for the manager." We waited for him to follow with the counteroffer, but the salesman just sat there staring at us. Finally, we asked what the counter was. The salesman simply reiterated that our first offer wasn't enough.

We were stupefied. They actually expected that we would continue to raise our offer, as many times as needed, until we hit a price that was acceptable to them. I asked my friend, "Why don't you offer $20,001?"

The salesman replied, "We can do that if you like, but we'll all be here for a very long time."

They actually expected us to bid against ourselves—not a great negotiating strategy. Our response was "Not likely," and we departed. What a Dingus! No movable goal on their side? Take a hike.

My second car purchase was for an elderly relative, who was unable to leave his home and needed a car for his live-in nurse. This meant I got to turn the tables on the sales team. Just as the salesman had to get everything approved by his manager, I had to phone my relative for approval. Was that fun! Every time the salesman would come in with a counteroffer, I could shake my head and say, "Boy, I don't know if he's gonna go for that." The dealership clearly didn't encounter this kind of one-upmanship much, and they had a hard time dealing with it. But the balance that I achieved through that technique led to a great final price.

When I contrasted that experience with my first negotiation, it made it very clear how useless it is to be stuck in an unbalanced negotiation. With my friend's attempted car purchase, the balance was missing—the dealership expected us to be flexible and move our position, while they intended to keep saying no until we had given in sufficiently. But that led only to my friend walking out the door. To negotiate successfully, both sides have to be willing to play by the same set of rules.

In your own negotiations, make sure that the balance exists—and I mean that both ways. Both you and the representative on the other side should have equal amounts of power over the agreement.

Going for the Win-Win

Consider again the car-buying story. When you're negotiating with the dealer, you have the same general goal: a car will change hands. You want to buy a car without getting ripped off. He wants to *sell* a car without getting ripped off. What's a win-win here? A car gets sold. That isn't so hard, is it?

When beginning any kind of negotiation, enter with the expectation that some kind of win-win solution is achievable. That expectation leads to results. When the other party can see that you are honestly making a best effort, he will be more willing to work with you toward a good solution. On the other hand, a Dingus starts from the premise that he will get exactly what he wants, even if it is at the total expense of the opposite party. That isn't a negotiation! And not only is it dumb from a business perspective, it also has an aroma that the other party will pick up fast. Once he's gotten a whiff of it, he's very unlikely to bargain in good faith. He will be on the defensive.

While you negotiate, periodically extract yourself from the depths of the discussion and try to view things from the other party's point of view. How would a third party view the progress of the negotiation? Are you coming across with the win-win attitude? Or are you being a Dingus?

The win-win attitude never means that you should accept a compromise that is not in the best interest of your team or the company in general. That isn't winning either. It simply means that you might have to do a little bit more work to get all your points across. As we discussed earlier, smart people should be able to look at a set of facts and arrive at a similar conclusion. Sometimes people might have personal biases that they need to set aside, but when that's done, everyone should be able to agree that the conclusion is logical. It's all a matter of making sure that all the facts are visible and understood.

Remember: when you come out on the "win" side of a win-lose solution, it might seem like victory to you. But when the other side doesn't have anything to gain by sticking with the solution, it's ultimately doomed to fail and you'll have to start all over again. Don't get yourself caught in that cycle. Negotiate to a win-win solution and—shockingly!—everyone wins.

Getting Respect from the Boss

Let's talk about your boss. Earlier in the book, we discussed the need to not only accomplish what he needs done, but to do it in a way that reflects well on him. Remember, the better the light you cast on your boss, the better his chances for advancement, and the better the chances of you moving up into his position!

But as you know from being a boss yourself, it isn't just about his needs. You also want to work in a way that fosters the best possible relationship between the two of you and enhances your mutual respect. That means, you're not just managing your people, you're also …

Chapter 12: Managing the Boss

The importance of the relationship you build with your boss cannot be overstated. No one can do more to advance or hinder your career than he can. As I said in the introduction to this book, regardless of your boss's management style, good or bad, you can still learn from him. And learning is always a good thing.

Keep in mind that when I use the word *boss* here, I am primarily referring to the person to whom you directly report. However, in many ways this information will apply to your higher-level superiors as well. Let's get started.

Learning His Communication Style

Most bosses are all about results. That's a welcome trait. As the competent manager you are, you should be able to wow your boss with your ability to get actual work accomplished by your team. But every boss has some degree of sensitivity toward how you handle the relationship from your end. Improperly done, you can set the relationship up for disaster, regardless of how well you actually deliver results. Adjusting to your boss's operation and interaction requirements is vital to your survival. But whatever your boss prefers, it doesn't make him a "good" or "bad" boss. It simply indicates his preferred communication style.

Discussions

If you haven't already done so, start taking note of what kind of communication style your boss prefers, and what styles seem to turn him off. Some bosses are very detail-oriented, and they enjoy hearing all the juicy details of every step of your current projects. Others want the executive summary and don't want you wasting their time with any more than the most general details of a given subject. Still others don't want to know anything about a topic at all unless it requires some action on their part. If that's the case, don't mistake his attitude for actual disinterest in your activities. Take it as a sign of trust that you can handle things, and that he knows you'll alert him when his time is really needed.

How can you learn how much detail your boss needs? Start with the summary, and then begin going into more detail. Watch for eyes glazing over, an attention shift to something going on out the window, or sudden interest in his email or cell phone. It won't take you long to zero in on his preferred level of detail. At the next briefing, give him that level of detail and stop. If the boss wants more information, he'll ask. Fill him in, and next time, assume that he generally desires a bit more detail and adjust your style to fit. Otherwise, stick with the level you've established.

Reports

What about written communications, such as reports? Those can be a bit trickier. You need to play to multiple levels, because your report may be "read" by a variety of people other than your boss. Of course, the word *read* is in quotes here, because many people who should read your report simply won't. At most, they will skim it. Therefore, it's important to include an "Executive Summary" section at the top that details the key elements of the report in one paragraph—which some also probably won't read. (There's only so much you can do.)

If your boss does read your reports, you don't want him to come back to you requesting more information. It isn't as easy for him to make the request, or for you to fulfill it, than when you're talking face-to-face. Lean toward providing a little more detail than you would in your face-to-face discussions. The keywords can be skimmed more easily in your report than when you're speaking.

Independence

Next, learn how much independence your boss wishes you to have. Some bosses want to give the official sign-off on much more of your work than others do. If you are starting from a position of trust, he may be perfectly happy to let you fly on your own unless you feel you need assistance. If you're a newcomer, he may want to keep a closer eye on you for a while. When you first start working with your boss, simply ask him what he prefers.

Despite whether he wants you to be more or less independent, however, it is vital to stay close to the level that he indicated he prefers. Don't stray much higher or lower than that point. If you come to a hands-off boss for approval far more frequently than he deems necessary, he's going to think you're overly burdensome and incapable of independent thought. If you seize more independence than he wishes, however, he's going to think you're a loner and maybe a bit out of control. Stick close to the level he wants, and you will, over time, earn additional independence.

Surprise! Here's a Blindside!

Nothing will please your boss less than getting blindsided by his boss or someone from another department. We discussed early on that you can't expect to be up-to-the-minute current on everything happening in your area, and there's no reason to feel that you have to keep your boss up to that level either. That's too big a burden on your own people and on you. Carefully pick the items of interest, and present them in an appropriate time frame.

But you must avoid the blind side. Clearly, any major developments are good candidates for a quick update to the boss. So are more minor issues that have direct negative implications for other departments or for customers. Ensure that should your boss get a call from one of his affected peers, or from his own boss, he's ready with at least a little bit of information on the subject. He will look like a completely out-of-touch moron if his response to an angry or critical call is "I don't know what you're talking about." And that won't reflect too well on you, either.

My methodology for these situations is to stick my head in his door with words like "Hey, I need to give you a quick heads-up on a situation that's brewing." Before long, your boss will be trained to know what this entails. You're about to give him information he's going to need in the near future, and he'll understand that it's time for a short burst of real concentration. Give him the quick summary of what's going on, who's involved, what the likely outcomes may be, and what steps your team is taking to sort it out. Now, when your boss gets the crisis call from another stakeholder, he will appear totally in touch and right on top of things.

By the way, when you pop into your boss's office for these situations—or any other—don't assume that, just because the door is open, he's ready to engage in conversation with you. Some bosses might be, and you'll learn if that's the case with yours. But always assume otherwise. My standard wording is "Hey, I've got a couple of things to go over with you. Let me know as soon as you've got a few minutes." He will appreciate you giving him the flexibility to prioritize you into his other happenings.

Making Complaints

Nobody likes a whiner. It's okay to have problems or complaints. But if one of your people constantly comes to complain unconstructively to you, how soon before you start hiding under the desk to avoid him? Don't fill that role for your boss either.

When you raise an issue with your boss, do it in a constructive manner. (You should be encouraging your people to operate the same way.) Spend some time before the meeting thinking through possible causes and solutions, even if the ability to implement the suggestion is completely outside your scope of control. When you have your discussion, your thoughtful analysis of the causes and solutions will change your boss's perception of the meeting from "How can I get out of here?" to "There are some good ideas here."

If you can't resolve an issue on your own, that's presumably because your boss is in a better position to actually act on the information you're discussing. It may require meetings with his own boss or peers, but he can probably work to fix your complaint. Work together with him to come up with a clear plan of attack. When the problem is finally fixed, a lot of people win, because the problem was most likely shared by other teams that aren't under your management. Nice job.

The Dingus whines and moans. Managers solve problems.

Don't Save the Punch Line

When you have problematic information to share with your boss, relating it in typical storytelling language is not likely to go over well. Even if you keep the story brief, your boss is going to start getting antsy to know where the story is going.

"First we did this. Then we did that. Then this happened, and then there was even more of that. But then someone did this and this, and …"

By this point, your boss is a nervous wreck. He isn't even listening to you much anymore. He's just wondering if everything came out all right or if someone is dead.

Always lead with the punch line.

"I need to let you know we had an accident in the factory, but everybody is fine and there won't be any negative effects on production. Do you want the details?"

Now he can relax. He'll let you know just how much extra detail he needs now, and what can wait until later.

Be Positive

It's so easy to be negative. For some reason, we humans have a tendency to immediately try to find fault with other people's ideas. And when someone asks if we can do something complicated, our brains are wired to jump into a mode of finding every potential obstacle and blurting them all out to everyone. Maybe it's that we don't like change. Maybe we're covering our butts. Who knows? The negative tendency is there regardless.

Trust me when I tell you that your boss doesn't want to hear all the reasons you can't get something done. He wants it done. Actually, he wants *you* to get it done. He wants you to find a way. Therefore, a response like "We could never get that done with all this other stuff going on!" is not the way to go. There's plenty of opportunity for a dose of reality—later.

Start out by being positive. "Yeah! I like that! We can do that!"

After all, you *can* do almost anything—assuming you're given the additional budget, people, time, or whatever else you need to make it happen. You aren't going to be asked to do something without the resources to do it or without having your priorities rearranged to accommodate it. Right?

So, again, start positive. Then you can turn the conversation, gently, back to the *CQBS* variables and M^2AT capabilities we've discussed and start to explore not *if* you can do it, but *how* you can. "Okay, let's examine what it's going to take to make this happen."

Now you can be realistic. "Can we put project X on the back burner to get to this now?" Or "I think if we shift a couple of workers over from project Y, we could handle this." Whatever it will take, start making suggestions, as primed by the *CQBS* and M^2AT equations.

In the end, the resources required to accomplish the boss's idea will amount to exactly the same thing whether you start positive or negative. But rather than making your boss (and everyone else) feel you're coming at the task from a negative point of view, show them that you're positive about it and eager to get it done. If the resources required to make it happen end up being too much to make the idea practical, everyone will see that. And it wasn't because you nixed the idea from the get-go.

In Boss We Trust

Simply stated, always believe that your boss is doing his best to represent you and your needs, even when that might not be apparent. Assume that he's fighting for you and your team, even if he's not winning some of those battles.

Remember the discussion in the "Sucking It Up" section in the previous chapter? If your boss has been given marching orders to follow, he should not be coming to you with statements like "This wasn't my decision." He should be supporting the decision as if it was his own. And if you disagree with the plan—and more so, you realize that he probably does too—understand from experience that he did his best for you.

At that point, when you've gotten marching orders of your own, the absolute worst thing you can do is to start hammering him about how displeased you are. He knows. And he's counting on you to not only be a good citizen, but to understand that he did what he could, even though he isn't saying it. So show that trust and respect. He'll fight even harder for you in the future.

Lookin' Good

Always consider how anything you do will make your boss look. You've already asked your workers to behave in all circumstances as if you were there watching. Keep the same thing in mind as you work. Whether you're leading a meeting, writing an email, preparing a presentation, or dropping in on a hallway conversation, will your boss be proud of your actions? Or are you making him look foolish?

When you accomplish a big goal, are you crediting your boss as the source of your success? Remember that even if he didn't agree with you about whatever path it was that turned out to be successful, he gave you the freedom and the trust to pursue it. That's worth crediting.

Remember, the better the light you cast on your boss, the better his chances for advancement … and the better the chances of him backing you to move up into his position!

Moving On

Now, let's take the final step and expand our discussion of communication to the rest of your working world. Much of what we've discussed about individual, group, and management communications will apply just as well when you have to interface ...

Chapter 13: Beyond the Team

Throughout this book, we've discussed a variety of techniques for interaction and communication with your subordinates, peers, and superiors. But these techniques are just as applicable to other working relationships—with other teams inside your company, and with outside vendors, suppliers, and customers.

As we approach the end of the book, let's take a look at a few more communication techniques that can be valuable for working beyond your team.

Making a Good First Impression

Many factors affect the impression you make when you first meet a new business contact: how you handle yourself during the discussion, your overall appearance and manner, and whether you really did use your hands to eat that spaghetti at lunch. But even before the meeting begins, you can give a *first* first impression with the manner in which you introduce yourself.

When you sit down for a business meeting with someone new, that person wants to know that he's about to work with a friendly, open team player. He wants to see that you take your work seriously, but also that you don't mind taking yourself a little more lightly.

You can begin to get this across in the few moments before the meeting even begins.

For example, what's the very first thing you say as you shake hands? The other party says, "Hi, I'm John Doe," and you reply with "And I'm Sam Smith. Nice to meet you"—which is great, except that you've forgotten that you met John Doe a year or two ago at some other meeting or conference. John recalls your meeting clearly, but to you he just wasn't that memorable. Not a good start.

Fortunately, that whoopsie is quite a bit easier to avoid than you might think. Many years ago, I noticed that talk-show host David Letterman always greeted his guests with a friendly "Nice to see you." I realized that he had devised a foolproof way to say hello without any implication of whether or not he had met that guest before. I adopted the trick immediately.

Next, don't rush to jam your business card into the hand you just shook. Watch for cues from the other parties, and follow their lead. If you're about to sit down with the Chinese or Japanese, for example, you will most likely proceed with a very formal exchange ceremony. But if you're meeting with a few Silicon Valley dot-com zillionaires wearing beat-up jeans, that level of formality probably won't mean much to them.

As the meeting begins, you have your next chance to make that early first impression. The group will probably go around the table to introduce themselves and their responsibilities. If you're meeting with high-level government officials, or to discuss a very serious situation, you'll want to retain a good degree of formality here. But in most situations, you'll be able to dial down on the officialism.

Instead of introducing yourself with "I'm the Senior Executive Manager of the customer services team," try something lighter like "I lead the customer services team" or even "I try to keep up with and take the credit for the cool stuff that my customer services team does." Everyone will still understand who you are without the formal title, and at the same time you'll get across all those points about being friendly, open, a team player, and capable of a little jocularity. The other parties will also see that you consider yourself to be on equal footing with your team members, instead of a dictator, and that you know your job is to let your team achieve its maximum effectiveness. That's a quality that carries over well to any business situation.

You Know That I Know That You Know

Whether you're speaking with individuals or groups, in a small or large setting, or presenting to thousands of people, it always pays to make your audience feel smart. Sometimes you'll know for certain that your audience is already acquainted with a particular topic. Other times you'll be in a situation where you can't be sure how much your audience knows. But no audience appreciates a speaker who talks down to them or makes them feel like out-of-touch dorks.

Make it a habit to introduce a topic with the *stated* assumption that your audience knows something about it, but the *actual* assumption that they do not. Note that this is quite different from asking, "Do you know about process X?" Even if the listener doesn't have a clue, his response to that will most likely be something like "A little." And that really means "I hadn't even heard the *name* process X until you said it, but I can say 'a little' and hope you explain enough about it while I pretend that everything you say is old hat to me." For obvious reasons, that response is especially likely in a group situation.

Why embarrass anyone like that? Instead, open your discussion with "I know you've heard about process X, wherein we take Y things and turn them into Z things by doing A and B." State that you know your audience is familiar with it, but then explain it as if they aren't. In a one-on-one or small group setting, the other parties will stop you or make it clear if they already understand. Otherwise, lay it all out. You'll get everyone up to at least the level of understanding you need to continue the discussion, and you'll make them all feel good in the process.

Dealing with Grenade Throwers

Let's deal with a completely different kind of outsider—one or more managers elsewhere in your company who were once responsible for your area, and who are now, consciously or unconsciously, undermining your work.

As a skilled manager, you may find yourself being brought in to handle a turnaround situation—in other words, to clean up someone else's mess. In some of these instances, the people responsible for the original mess will have been dismissed. If that's the case, they are now being paid to make messes at other fine establishments, and they are fully out of your hair.

But much of the time, at least some of the responsible parties will still be around somewhere inside your own company. If they're mostly benevolent, you may not have to deal with them further. But in the worst case, if they feel that your work will show them up or get them in trouble for accomplishing what they could not, they might begin to undermine you by providing conflicting information to your boss, or to his boss—at whatever point up the food chain that your paths cross.

This really happens. In fact, I have been in this exact situation twice in my own career. In both cases, I was tasked with fixing a broken product whose previous leadership had been moved off to another area outside my boss's organization.

Keep the Boss Informed

The first time I was brought in to turn around a product, we immediately realized that the previous leaders, who still had connections to the Big Boss, were constantly feeding him information that undermined our work. "Those new people are saying they're going to double the performance of the product. That's impossible. It's a waste of time to even try."

The Big Boss was getting information on our progress before we had a chance to report it to him, and the information he was getting was spun drastically in a way that wasn't helpful to us. My boss and I were forced to constantly defend ourselves. Even positive reports of our progress were preemptively quashed by bad information from the other side.

We responded by setting up daily meetings with the Big Boss, where we'd share exactly what we were doing and why we were doing it. We made it a point to ensure that he would hear about our progress from us first. From that point on, when someone from the previous team would try to give us negative press, the Big Boss would already have the correct version of the story. He was quick to put the previous leadership in their place, and soon they stopped attempting to undermine our work. After that, our turnaround went much more smoothly.

Get Everyone Involved

When I encountered the same situation again, years later, I adopted the same plan immediately. But this time I took it one step further. My team began having regular meetings with the people who had previously been in charge of our products. We would give the previous leaders complete status reports, ask them for advice, and run our future plans by them to get feedback and support.

The result was remarkable. Because we got them involved on a regular basis, the previous leadership became an extended part of our team. And because we asked them for advice and support, they couldn't very well turn on us behind our backs. Most importantly, by making them a part of our extended team, we were able to get real support from them when we needed extra voices to back us up on budget or hiring requests. The old team turned out to be a truly positive resource.

When you find yourself in a situation like this, take a proactive approach. Own the communications flow yourself. And what's that old saying? "Keep your friends close, but keep your enemies closer."

Communicating with Customers

If you work for a start-up company, you may have the luxury of not having any customers yet. Nobody has formally paid you money (other than your investors!). You don't have any type of product on the market. Lucky you! That means no support headaches. Nobody screaming at you to fix anything. Nobody demanding a new feature *yesterday*. You are free to focus your attention entirely on developing the initial version of whatever product or service you intend to offer.

Fast-forward a few months. You're now officially in business. You've started selling to those long-sought-after customers, and the money is starting to flow. Unfortunately, so are the headaches. Now you've got people out there who are actually relying on your product or service. They paid good money, and they expect everything to be perfect. And they also feel that they have the right to dictate your future direction. What a distraction!

Customers Are a Terrible Thing

Suddenly, all that wonderful focus you had in the beginning is being diluted by the problems and suggestions of your newfound customer base. Customers are a terrible thing—they make you focus on and do things that you might rather not. It's frustrating when you have to divert so much time to these tasks, especially if you still have a long list of things you wish you had done the first time around.

You have two choices here. One, achieve utter perfection in your very first pass at your new product or service. That way, you'll be able to avoid most of the requests and complaints. Of course, you may never get to market, either, and you're pretty certain to run out of funds before a good revenue flow gets going. Good luck with that!

Alternatively, you can choose to appreciate your customers for what they're doing—telling you exactly what you need to do to provide more value. When you fix problems and provide the things they specifically request, you help them, provide more value for what they're paying, and increase your company's value at the same time. Everybody wins.

Get Them Involved

The key point here is to include some of your likely customers early in the development process. This is true even if you are a well-established company beginning work on a new product. Get your customers into your shop and pick their brains clean. But don't stop there. Bring them in as often as you can—if not in person, by telephone or video conference—to see your work as it progresses and offer ideas for fine-tuning your new product.

Consulting with your customers in advance will stop you from marching down completely invalid paths, providing overly complex solutions, or adding features that get in the way instead of adding true value. And it won't take you any longer to develop your solution. Indeed, by avoiding all the backtracking, false starts, and duplicated efforts, you will save significantly in the long run.

Act Proactively

No matter how good you are, it's impossible to satisfy 100 percent of your customers 100 percent of the time. Accept the fact that you'll have to speak with a few of the peeved ones occasionally. Unpleasant as they might sound, do not avoid these interactions. In fact, the conversation with an unhappy customer is very similar to the meeting with an employee to deliver an unsatisfactory performance review. On the surface, these conversations appear to have all the excitement of a good rope burn. But if you handle them deftly, you have the opportunity to turn the situation around and transform a customer from miserable to delighted.

First, go out of your way to contact the customer right away. Don't make your customer come looking for you. If your company has more than a couple dozen employees who all know each other, it can be very difficult for your customers to locate the right person in charge. And as soon as he gets lost in your support voicemail limbo, or struggles to push something up the line through your sales channel, your customer may give up on both you and your company—except, of course, he'll be happy to tell his friends all about it.

I first learned this lesson back in college, when I was supervising one of my city's swimming pools. A swimmer's car was unfortunate enough to receive a car wash from a poorly aimed lawn sprinkler ... while the windows were open. I jumped into action, and I *thought* I did everything right. I apologized. I sent a crew of lifeguards to the car with towels. And I gave the swimmer the names and phone numbers of everyone to call at the city offices the next morning.

Shutting Up

Good for me! But later that day, when I described the situation to my manager, he asked, "Wouldn't it have been easier to take his information and have someone from the city call him?" Duh. I put the onus to communicate on my customer, when I should have kept it in our hands.

Keep Your Eyes Open

Being proactive also means staying on the lookout for customers who are getting into trouble and might need some personal contact with your team. Make sure that your service and sales teams know that you want to be brought into the loop as early as possible when a customer relationship might be degenerating. If you have some sort of CRM system that will allow you to automatically generate notifications or reports of big issues out in the wild, keep an eye on that. If not, perhaps your support teams can provide a weekly report of customers who have had particular difficulty. Whatever you do, do something.

I once worked for a large company that had a link on every product Web page that said, "Click here to submit a comment, suggestion, or complaint about this product." Given that this company had literally millions of customers, those links got an awful lot of clicks. I was the head of one of the products—and guess who actually got to read and respond to those clicks? That's right. The comments weren't sent to frontline support or a marketing intern. They were targeted directly to me.

I spent an hour or two every day sorting through comments and responding to those that really needed it. What an eye-opening experience! There was a direct pipeline from our customers to my email inbox, with no filter. Some customers took the opportunity to question the family lineage of everyone on my team, but others sent fantastic suggestions that genuinely helped us improve our products. And instead of just reading and deleting the complaints, I took them as an opportunity to salvage a bad experience.

In one case, I messaged back and forth a number of times with a single customer. He had started out very unhappy, but I had given him lots of help, comped him a few items, and responded positively to his suggestions—even committing to him that some of his feature requests would be in the next release. His mood was steadily improving.

It is important to note here that nowhere in the "make a comment" link did it indicate that the correspondence would be sent to the Vice President in charge of the product group. And in my messages with the customer, I simply signed them with my first name—no title. After a few days, as our exchanges were coming to a close, I actually called him on the phone to thank him again for his feedback. We had a conversation that went pretty much like this:

Customer: "Thanks so much for all the information. You are cool. And when you get a chance to talk to The Man, tell him you deserve a raise!"

Me: "Thanks! I appreciate that. But just so you know, I am The Man."

Customer: "Huh?"

Me: "I'm actually the VP in charge of product development. I handle these comments personally to make sure we're making good use of all the information that people send."

Customer: "That is really cool. I thought you were just some customer support person. That's cool that your company feels we're that important."

I've paraphrased, but the customer did say "cool" a lot. We had saved him some frustration and made him a lot happier. And it was cool for me, too. We got some great future product direction out of the exchange. And once again, you can bet my customer told his friends about the experience.

Don't Give Up

When a customer problem continues to go sour, do whatever you can to salvage it. It costs far more to attract a new customer than it does to retain one, so it makes sense to go the extra mile. Factor in the pyramid effect when your departing customers tell all their friends, coworkers, neighbors, and relatives how lousy you are, and the damage can be immense.

Still, at some point, with some customer, you're going to feel that you've exhausted every logical option. You're going to ask yourself, "What else can we honestly do here that will help?" That's when you have to change your thinking—and stop limiting yourself to things that make sense. Sometimes you need to go a little further, to things that *don't* seem logical on the surface.

We talked before about news channels that throw helicopters at news stories that don't really deserve them. You can do the same. In fact, I call it "putting the helicopter on the scene."

Send one of your best people out to the customer's site. Send yourself! Talk to the customer in person. See his problems. Feel his pain. He will appreciate it more than you can imagine. No, showing up and listening to him may not do anything more to actually solve the problem, but the increased personalization will buy you credibility and time to get things right. You'll also have a chance to let him click on that "make a comment or suggestion" button in person and tell you everything that's on his mind. That will further improve your relationship, and probably help out the product in the long run as well.

And here's something I've experienced repeatedly, thanks to that helicopter. More often than not, when you visit the customer, you will see something new—something the customer didn't think to report, or an additional clue about whatever it is that's making his life unpleasant. You'll be able to funnel information back to your team that will help get this customer back up and running quicker than you otherwise would have. That's a win for all of us.

Human Resources

If your company is anything larger than tiny, your Human Resources department wields a ton of power. The people there have the ability to make your life and job much more pleasant—or utterly unbearable. These are people with whom you need to consciously build a relationship. I failed to properly understand this early in my career, and I certainly paid the price.

When you arrive at a new company, get to know your HR team as early and as well as you can. Go out to lunch with them, and do everything in your power to make them feel comfortable with you and glad to have you on board. Service organizations in general, and HR teams specifically, have more than enough crap to deal with from people like you. Try to be one of the managers with whom they actually like to work, rather than the Dingus they try to run away from.

Anytime you see signs of an HR issue arising within your team, alert your HR rep as soon as possible. And when you need to speak with them—whether they call you or you call them—don't settle for phone calls if their location is within walking distance. Instead, tell them, "Hey, I'll just pop over there and we'll talk in person." This is actually a good idea for any team with which you need to build rapport.

A good HR team will be stocked with people who see their job as trying to help you be successful by maximizing the *human resources* on your team. I don't necessarily mean giving you more people—I mean making the most of what you have through appropriate hiring, training, compensation, bonuses, and other techniques. When the HR team has needs, listen to them as you'd listen to your own workers. While you may not always agree with their policies, working within the system will get you a lot further than antagonism. Their job is to help *everyone* succeed. Let them do it.

The Offshoring Cycle

In my management lifetime, I have seen the love affair with offshoring begin three times. And I've seen the nasty divorce about two and a half times. (As of this writing, much of the country seems to be pulling back from the latest cycle.) At the beginning of each cycle, companies fall for the promise of productive work performed quickly at a fraction of onshore rates. And in a few cases, they have some degree of success with this option. In many other cases, however, the dream goes unfulfilled and is eventually abandoned.

Some companies practice offshoring as standard company policy, while others have adopted a "when hell freezes over" approach. You can make your own decision; I will not be discussing the political aspects of offshore work here. I will cover only some key points that you should examine if you are considering sending some of your work offshore.

Note that when I say *offshoring*, I am generally using the standard meaning of "sending to another country." However, many of the same points and caveats apply when you send any work to a group outside your own—to an outside vendor, and even sometimes to another department within your own company.

Eligible Offshorables

The first rule of offshoring is to not contract out any products or services that are considered the Company Jewels. If you have ancillary products, or you want to dabble around in some new area without making a big commitment of your key onshore people, that's one thing. Offshoring can also make sense for truly short-term projects, as long as you don't mind losing most or all of the knowledge that went into their creation.

But you are asking for trouble if you offshore your bread-and-butter products, any task that involves close-held company secrets, or a project for which you need to retain the source talent and knowledge. Entrusting those projects to anyone outside your close scope of control is, to be blunt, an absolutely terrible idea. Even if there seems to be cost advantages to sending out that work, the long-term cost-benefit analysis will never be in your favor. Keep those projects and their associated staff close to you.

Secondly, never, ever offshore a mess. Before you send any existing project outside your team, consider the shape that the project is in and ask yourself what you are really trying to gain by offshoring it. If the project has somehow run amok—major quality problems, extensive delays—or it's just a mess in general, do not send it offshore with the hope of somehow cleaning it up. The complexities inherent to offshoring will almost certainly negate any possibility of improvement. Clean up the mess in-house before you proceed with any other changes.

Buy-In Is Key

So, you're thinking about sending out a project that meets the eligibility criteria we just discussed. Now it's time to get the whole management team to buy in to your plan. Note that this buy-in is not optional. If you choose to skip this step, you will not get the results you desire.

Once again, it's time to make use of the listening and negotiating practices we've already discussed. You must have unanimous support from your team before you proceed. Without it, someone will work to undermine the project. It may not be conscious, but someone will think the work should have gone to him or the product itself is a bad idea. Or maybe he simply has an inherent distaste for moving jobs to another country. But if you don't get him on board, it won't matter why. Without the complete support of your entire team, you're doomed. You will have enough problems keeping things coordinated with another team that's a dozen time zones away. Having to keep things in hand in your own time zone as well is a distraction you don't need.

And remember: smart people should be able to look at a set of facts and, setting aside personal biases, agree on a reasonable conclusion. If you can't get everyone on board with your central plan, can you be sure you're doing the right thing?

Making It Work

Once your team has bought into the idea, start examining logistics. If your company already has facilities offshore, that's probably where you'll be headed. In that case, there should already be procedures in place for coordinating the work, which will help you avoid a number of pitfalls. If you're going to be contracting with an outside shop, however, you need to do everything in your power to pick a winner. Do your research, and be thorough! Use every contact you have and dig up every piece of information you can find to give yourself the best shot at success.

Delegate a member of your in-house team to lead the effort. And by "lead the effort," I mean *lead the effort*. The person you choose cannot hold a weekly status call with the remote outfit and then forget about it for the other thirty-nine hours of the week. If you do expect to stop at that level of involvement, don't bother starting in the first place. You need real, constant contact with the remote facility to keep things going as planned. Otherwise, I guarantee you will experience the following problems:

- Confusion about requirements. "Oh, you wanted it to do that?"
- Work outside the required scope. "Yes, we know you wanted just that one thing, but we thought this would be a nice addition."
- Incorrect and creative cost accounting. That's a nice way of saying "being double or triple billed." My team once discovered that the offshore company, which had been billing us for a group of ten engineers on our task, had exactly two people doing the work. I've also been billed for a group of workers as if they were working full-time on my project, and then discovered that another corporation was also being billed for the same workers at the same time.
- Quality far below expectations. Enough said.
- Apparent productivity that's nowhere close to what you were expecting. I once asked my project team to round up the speed and quality metrics of an offshore group I'd just inherited. Not only was the offshore group performing far below regular norms, they were below the norms expected even on government projects. Now that's bad!

The best way to deflect these dangers is to have someone totally involved in the effort, right up to his neck. He will need to travel frequently—or, even better, live in the remote location. Your minimum goal should be for him to spend 50 percent of his time at the remote site. Taking status updates by conference call at 10 PM won't cut it—your team leader would still be interfacing with only one or two lead people from the remote group, and it's incredibly difficult to build and maintain a motivated team that way. With such minimal contact, it's even more difficult to get the straight story about what's going on. Plus, the leader's presence on-site will ensure that the project is getting the attention it deserves and that you are being billed appropriately.

What's more, it's imperative that your team leader can speak the native language of the remote team. I know it isn't necessarily easy to find a truly capable leader who also happens to be bilingual, but I've never seen a successful offshoring operation without one. That one person makes all the difference in the success. That's because, with him in place, you can treat the remote team exactly as if they were back home in the onshore group. Your leader can work directly with any of the team members. He can make quick corrections. He will know the team, they will know him, he can speak to them about higher-level project issues, and he can get the straight story. But at the end of the day, he works for you, not them.

Why It Doesn't Work

So, I've just given you some tips on how to make offshoring work. But as I also pointed out right at the start, it usually doesn't. Why not? Why does offshoring keep encountering these love/hate cycles every ten years or so?

The answer ends up being pretty simple: offshoring is almost never as good a deal as you think it will be. The communication problems are huge, the support required by your management and project teams is often difficult to muster, quality and productivity usually don't come close to your expectations, your employees and customers grow frustrated with the quality of the service or product, and costs tend to increase quickly.

At one company in my past, a friend of mine on another team set up an offshore shop to take on a new project. Initially, the cost per worker was projected at about 15 percent of the cost of a similar worker back home. Sounded great! Even if the people overseas were only half as productive as home-side workers, they could get the new project done at a substantially lower cost. But then reality set in. The overhead costs of coordination, communication, travel, and new facilities ate into the margin. And no one counted on the flood of other companies showing up to hire "cheap" workers in that country at the same time. By the end of the first year, the cost for an offshore worker had more than doubled to about 33 percent of the cost of a home-side worker, not including the increased overhead and the confusion it caused at home. The cost model had been trashed.

Here's the bottom line: don't offshore something just because you think (or hope) it will save money. Make sure that everything about the decision makes sense.

The Consultant Conundrum

Even the best companies will, from time to time, have some big problems that it seems no one can figure out how to solve. So management decides to bring in an outside consultant to figure it out. Sometimes they'll hire someone without knowing exactly what the problem is. Sometimes they don't know whether there's a problem at all—but they figure something is going on, so they hire a consultant to come in and survey things for general improvement.

Straightforward enough, right? The consultant arrives, examines the situation, interviews a ton of people, applies analysis born of years of experience at analyzing other companies, and writes a lengthy report that tells upper management what corrections should

Shutting Up

be made. A lengthy report—and an expensive one. Companies have been known to spend tens, even hundreds of thousands of dollars on these investigations and findings. Remember that you're paying the consultant to point out all your warts, and he'll do his best to find as many of them as he can—even if some are questionable.

Here's what's really sad about this: in most cases, the supposedly unknown problems are already common knowledge. And almost as often, so are the solutions. Maybe the upper-management team doesn't have a clue. But somewhere in the organization, there's someone who deals with this problem on a regular basis. And, chances are, he has a pretty good idea of what kind of pain it's causing and how it should be fixed.

But if the problems and solutions are so obvious, why did someone have to hire the consultant in the first place? Maybe it's because nobody at the higher level bothered to ask anybody else about it. (You'd think that asking around a little would be a pretty easy way to save some money, not to mention all the lost time waiting for the results to come in!) However, unbelievably, sometimes the management team *already knows* about the very problems or solutions they're seeking through the consultant's services.

What the ... ? If that's the case, why on earth are they wasting time and money on the consultant?

Well, why is the government always forming task forces to dream up solutions when everyone already knows how to solve the problem? Politics. CYA. Deniability. Whatever. Most likely it's because when the task force comes up with an unpopular or expensive recommendation, the person who originated the task force can deflect the blame. "It's not my idea! The consultant said so!"

Unfortunately, the same thing happens in the business world. We bring in someone else—an independent, unbiased third party—to come to the same conclusion we all know is true anyway. Then we can't be held to blame. Smart ... at least from a certain point of view.

Again, some of these third-party involvements are undertaken simply because nobody thought to check with the people who might already know the answers. Fortunately, you know how to avoid mistakes like that. But if you ever find yourself in the position to debate the necessity of the outside consultant for issues like these, speak up. Have some pride in yourself and your team, and do what needs to be done.

Chapter 14: Summing It All Up

We've just covered a heck of a lot of material in a pretty short time. It may take some thinking to assimilate it all, but let's take a moment to consider what we've learned. In fact, let's go back to the beginning and try to condense it all into its most important point.

If there's only one concept you take away from the discussion in this book, take the very first one: *Know when to shut up.* Listen, listen, and then listen some more. Ask open questions and make brief comments if necessary to get the other person's words flowing again, but then return to the key point and *shut up again.* Even when you think it's your turn to speak, try waiting a little longer. Be absolutely certain that you've ferreted out all of the points that the other person wants to make. Only then should you begin to make any substantive analysis or comments.

Nobody will ever fault you for listening too much. But they'll be quick to criticize or resent you when you don't allow them to get out what they really want to say.

When you demonstrate that listening is more important to you than speaking, you send the message that you truly want to understand other people. That understanding comes only when you learn that what you have to say is never more important than what someone else has to say to you.

Holding your tongue also communicates a basic comprehension of how teams need to work together to be successful. No single member of a team is more important than any other member—most especially you. Everyone has a different job to do, and everyone must perform their functions in order for the team to succeed. We, as managers, aren't doing any real work. We're doing meta-work—work about work. Our job is to make it easy for the real work to get done. Try to maintain that perspective.

Now, take what you've learned and start mentoring others to be their best as well. Give them a copy of this book, or simply have a discussion. You can help improve everyone around you. Remember that making your boss look good reflects well on you. Helping your subordinates do well reflects even better.

But while we're at it, why use what you've learned here only in your working life? Why limit your new listening behavior to the office and your coworkers? Your friends and family deserve this treatment as well. Whether you're acting as a boss, a friend, a spouse, or a parent, always try to convey a sense of equality when you're speaking with someone else. Listen closely first.

I hope you've enjoyed consuming these tips as much as I did in saving and compiling them. Live long, prosper, may the force be with you, and don't be a Dingus.

From the Author:

If you would like to learn more or contact me, or are interested in interviews or speaking engagements, head on over to shuttingup.com.

www.ingramcontent.com/pod-product-compliance
Lightning Source LLC
Chambersburg PA
CBHW030922180526
45163CB00002B/430